MARGUERITE YOURCENAR IN COUNTERPOINT

C. Frederick Farrell, Jr.
Edith R. Farrell

UNIVERSITY
PRESS OF
AMERICA

LANHAM • NEW YORK • LONDON

Reprinted by permission of Farrar, Straus and Giroux, Inc. Excerpts from **A Coin in Nine Hands** by Marguerite Yourcenar, translated from the French by Dori Katz. Translation copyright © 1982 by Farrar, Straus and Giroux, Inc. Excerpts from **Fires** by Marguerite Yourcenar, translated from the French by Dori Katz. Translation copyright © 1981 by Farrar, Straus and Giroux, Inc.
Reprinted by permission of The Macmillan Company. The untitled poem by W. B. Yeats from **The Variorum Edition of the Poems of W.B. Yeats,** edited by Peter Allt and Russell K. Alspach, The Macmillan Company, 1957.

This book is dedicated

to

Marguerite Yourcenar

on the occasion of her

eightieth birthday

June 8, 1983

The one who's wise is not weighed down by age.
His mind stays keen. A prophet and a sage,
A messenger from God, who, by his pen,
Serves, for all his life, his fellow men.

in **La Couronne et la Lyre**
from **Florilegium** by Strobius

Table of Contents

Preface

Marguerite Yourcenar in Counterpoint is a collection of essays written over a period of five years—1978-1982—that adopts a non-traditional viewpoint. The first four essays focus upon some of the early, often less widely read works of a woman whose international reputation rests largely upon two historical novels, **Mémoires d'Hadrien** and **L'Oeuvre au noir.** Both of these have often been described as "magisterial," a cold word suggesting the philosophy lesson. The present volume will concentrate on her as an artist. Images, themes, and structure will receive greater emphasis than ideas, although these will not be neglected. The last three essays are intended primarily to illustrate lesser known aspects of her writings and include examples from all stages of her career. Throughout, there has been an attempt to show relationships among her different works.

Our original aim in writing these articles was three-fold: 1) to bring to the attention of the English-speaking world a major figure in twentieth-century letters who has been an American citizen since 1947; 2) to encourage admirers of **Hadrien** and **L'Oeuvre au noir** to read and enjoy her earlier works; 3) to counteract certain common misconceptions about her and her work, such as her supposed neglect of women.

Three of the essays in this book have been published in scholarly journals: "The Art of Rewriting" in **L'Esprit créateur,** XIX, 2 (Summer, 1979); "Mirrors and Masks" in **Papers on Language and Literature,** XVII, 3 (Summer, 1981); and **"Feux:** Structure and Meaning" in **Kentucky Romance Quarterly,** XXIX, 1, 1982. They have been revised for this volume. "The Essays: The Work That Is—The Work That Might Have Been" was read at the Modern Language Association convention in New York in December, 1981, while "Antigone Twice Retold" was presented at the Georgia Colloquium '82 in Athens, Georgia, April, 1982. The other two essays appear here for the first time.

All of these studies are based on the French texts. The quotations are given in English to reach a wider audience, but the references are given to a French edition (the **Pléïade** for the definitive version of the works included in the first volume) and to the English where available, e.g. (Pl 1027; E 41). Quotations which do not have a reference to an English edition are our own translations.

It is hoped that **Marguerite Yourcenar in Counterpoint** will suggest new ways of approaching this author, known to many as the first woman elected to the Academie francaise.

We wish to thank the Graduate School of the University of Minnesota, which supported our research with a Grant-in-aid; the librarians of the University of Minnesota, Morris, especially Barabara Mc Ginnis, for their help in assembling the needed documentation; and the staff of the Computer Center of the University of Minnesota, Morris, especially Angel Lopez, Lynn Schulz, and Pam Gades for their assistance while we prepared the manuscript.

The Woman and Her Work

Marguerite Yourcenar is a French writer who is an American citizen. She is a woman, and a woman who by-passed most of the rituals of Paris literary life, yet she was elected to the Académie française. She is in the mainstream of modern French letters, although she has never accomodated her subjects or her style to the newest literary fashions. She lives in Northeast Harbor, a small village on Mount Desert Island off the coast of Maine, yet her books are set in many countries -- Greece, Spain, China, America, Belgium, India, and Italy, among others--and in many times--Graeco-Roman, the Renaissance, the twentieth-century, and in the mythical past which is the eternal present. Her characters include princes, peasants, gods and outcasts, the learned and the illiterate; they are monks or soldiers, housewives or queens, philosophers or businessmen, artists or prostitutes. There are Christians, Jews, Moslems, Hindus, Taoists, and Buddhists. Her milieus range from castles to country cottages, from centers of power to desolate outposts of civilization, from heavily ornamented homes to natural settings where only one human being--or none at all--intrudes upon the solitude of nature.

The woman who writes these works is equally complex. She says, as did her character, Zeno, "I am one, but many are within me." She has been painted as a hermit. This picture stresses the isolation of her island home in contrast to the literary centers of Paris or New York. It emphasizes her being in a foreign country and seems to assume that because her activities are not recorded in the newspapers that she is always alone. A closely allied image of her, that of the philosopher, makes her almost a disembodied mind. Growing out of a profound respect for her accomplishments, this portrait underscores her grasp of many fields of scholarship--history, classics, philosophy, religion, and literary criticism. On the other hand, photographs often show her in her kitchen or her yard. They are intended to portray her as mistress of her home, a woman who enjoys cooking, bakes her own bread, and loves dogs and children--who feeds birds, looks out for Joseph (a ground squirrel who uses the bird bath at the same hour every day), and doesn't want to chase away the skunk who chose to make his home under her porch.

1

All of these images are true, but none is true by
itself. Marguerite Yourcenar encompasses all of these
characteristics and more. She was convinced early in
her life that she was intended to communicate to the
world. She has spoken of herself as a medium and as a
theater in whom dramas unfold. Much of her life has
been spent in perfecting the skills that will allow
her to do this to the very best of her ability. Virtually self-taught, she studied under tutors only until
she received her baccalauréat at the age of sixteen.
She has read and traveled widely to acquire the knowledge and the experience with life that enable her to
write her books.

Her life is not limited to literature, however,as
some would have us believe. Her home, filled as it is
with books,with mementos of her family and of her travels, and with carefully chosen works of art, is open
to her friends and neighbors. She writes her books
"when she has the time," but stops frequently to speak
to whoever might come by, such as the man who helps
her with her garden, and must set aside time each day
to deal with her voluminous correspondence.Her friends
are of all ages, countries, and stations in life, and
she does not believe that either distance or lapse of
time can destroy a friendship.

Her election to the French Academy was widely re-
ported in the world press, partly because the Academy
itself was in the throes of coping with adjustments to
the 1980's, where denial of membership to a woman because she was a woman seemed grotesque.The problem was
in reality three-fold: she had refused to apply in the
regular way; her nationality was in question; and she
was a woman. Traditionally those wishing to become one
of the "Forty Immortals" make a round of formal visits
to the Academicians to solicit their votes. Marguerite
Yourcenar, to whom ambition of this type is foreign,
did not even consider such a move. Instead, Jean d'Ormesson made the trip to Maine to ask her to allow him
to propose her name. She agreed only to write a letter
saying that she "would not be so impolite as to refuse
if elected." Some members objected to her being an
American citizen(she had not retained her French citizenship), but this objection was easily dealt with by
giving her dual citizenship. Long and acrimonious debate centered on the admissibility of a woman;the vote
had to be postponed. The President of the Republic,
Valéry Giscard d'Estaing, had made no secret of his

2

desire to see her in the Academy, but it finally took
no less a diplomat than Edgar Faure, himself an Academy member, to reconcile diametrically opposed views
and to treat bruised egos. On March 6, 1980, when word
came of her election, Marguerite Yourcenar was not at
home waiting for the telegram; she was getting ready
to board a ship for a cruise through the Caribbean.

In her formal acceptance speech, she disregarded,
for the most part, the furor that had surrounded her
election. She merely reminded the Academy that she
was not the first woman who had been worthy of being
chosen, and said that when women are placed on a ped-
estal, the men forget to offer them a "chair," referring to the forty numbered chairs in which the members sit when the Academy holds its regular sessions.
What brought this woman to such an historic moment?

She was born in Brussels in 1903, but was immediately registered as a French citizen and given the
name Marguerite Antoinette Jeanne Marie Ghislaine
Cleenwerk de Crayencour. Her father, Michel, a French-
man, and her mother, Fernande de Cartier de Marchienne
a Belgian, both belonged to old Flemish families. Ten
days after the child's birth, her mother died. It was
the constant presence of her father, however, not the
death of her mother, that had the greatest effect upon
the girl and the young woman. Although she was cared
for by maids and taught by a succession of tutors, it
was from her father that she got her taste for literature and philosophy, for Latin, Greek, and English. A
favorite evening's activity that they often shared
was reading aloud and discussing what they had read.
Among the books that they most enjoyed were those of
Tolstoy, Ibsen, and Shakespeare.

While she lives in a modest white frame house today, she spent her early childhood at Mont Noir--a cha-
teau built by her great-great-grandfather, not far from
the city of Lille. Just before the First World War, her
father--a man who placed little value on family tradi-
tion--sold the ancestral home. At the outbreak of the
war in September, 1914, the two of them found themselves
on the Belgian coast visiting friends. They escaped to
to England where they spent about a year. Later they
lived in Paris, the south of France, and Switzerland,
while taking trips elsewhere in Europe.

Having been accustomed to the nomadic life, Marguerite Yourcenar did not establish a permanent home

3

of her own until almost forty years later when, with
her friend, Grace Frick, she bought "Petite Plaisance"
'Small Pleasure,' in Maine. Here she has lived since
1950, but with frequent trips around the world: to Eu-
ope,Africa,South America, and Asia. After her father's
death in 1929, she allowed her older half-brother to
manage her inheritance.A friend of the family salvaged
about a fourth of it from the ensuing disaster.At that
that time she made a decision for which she still con-
gratulates herself: she broke with her family--its
bourgeois values and interests--and went to live in
Greece in order to find herself. She counted on having about ten years of freedom living on money left
her by her mother and then, she planned merely to see
what would happen.1

The coming of World War II and the coming to an
end of her fortune coincided in 1939. These two factors were to have a profound effect on her life. They
combined to induce her to accept an invitation from
Grace Frick, whom she had met in 1937, to come to the
United States. She planned to spend six months here
before returning to Greece, but when the six months
were over, Europe was no longer the same. Needing to
earn her living, for the first time,Marguerite Yourcenar accepted the position of part-time instructor at
Sarah Lawrence. She continued to teach there until
just after the publication of **Mémoires d'Hadrien** when
she resigned to devote herself full-time to writing.

She had begun her literary career at about four-
teen. Her first efforts were in verse, since, as she
wryly explained somewhere,prose seems to a young writer like an ocean in which one can very quickly drown.
Her father had her first two works printed privately,
and the two spent an enjoyable evening making anagrams
of Crayencour to find a pen name,Yourcenar, with which
to sign them. The first, **Le Jardin des Chimères** 'The
Garden of the Chimeras' (1921), is a long dramatic poem based on the Icarus legend, which attracted the attention of the Indian nobelist,Tagore, who invited her
to come to Bengal. This is one of the choices about
which she has wondered since, but also one of the many
chance happenings that determine a life. The second
book, **Les Dieux ne sont pas morts** 'The Gods Still

---

1. **Archives du nord** (Paris: Gallimard, 1977), p. 305.

4

Live' a collection of her adolescent poems, followed in 1922.

Although these two works lack the consummate artistry of the mature writer, they are nonetheless important, for they reveal many of the themes that will recur throughout her career: the importance of the sacred, the search for absolutes, the unimportance of material goals, the co-existence of the real and the imaginary, the accepting of the physical, spiritual, and intellectual as manifestations of a single human spirit, the relationship of man to the natural world, art as creation and reflection, the concept of the universe as one and, finally, the perfection of the self.

The decade 1929-1939 proved to be one of her most prolific. She published nine works in ten years. Essays in this book deal specifically with **Alexis, Denier du rêve (A Coin in Nine Hands), Feux (Fires),** and **Nouvelles Orientales** 'Oriental Tales.' Two other important ones should be noted briefly:**Les Songes et les sorts** 'Dreams and Destinies,' and **Coup de grâce.**

The first is an exploration of the unconscious source of both dreams and poetry through a recounting of a series of dreams experienced by the author and an introduction to the interpretation of dreams. **Coup de grâce,**published in 1939 on the eve of the Second World War, is a love story, a tragedy set in novel form, exhibiting the classical unities of "time,place,and danger." It involves three young people whose youth unfolds against a background of the antibolshevic skirmishes in Courland that followed the First World War. This description of disrupted lives was later to appear prophetic.

It is during this period, too, that she began her career as a translator. She is known in France for her translation of Virginia Woolf's **The Waves,** first published in 1937. Henry James' novel, **What Maisie Knew,** was also done at this time, although it did not appear until 1947. Translation from English and from both ancient and modern Greek is one of the leisure time activities in which Marguerite Yourcenar has engaged throughout her literary career. In 1940 she brought out translations and a critical introduction to the contemporary Greek poet, Constantine Cavafy, which were published as a book in 1958. In 1964, her collection of Negro Spirituals, **Fleuve profond, Sombre riviére** 'Deep River, Dark River' and, in 1969, her

5

translations of poems by her friend, Hortense Flexner, brought specifically American works to a French audience. **La Couronne et la lyre** 'The Crown and the Lyre,' is an anthology in verse of twelve centuries of ancient Greek poetry. She did these translations over a period of many years, at first solely for her own pleasure, but later with a view to choosing representative poems providing an overview of the changes in Greek civilization. Some specialists have commented that her poems in this volume at times surpass the originals in beauty.

Her teaching schedule, coupled with the distress of the war, bouts with illness, and the impossibility of her publishing in the Paris of the Occupation, all contributed to an interruption of her work during the decade of the forties. She wrote some plays, which were collected and printed some years later. These, and a series of articles printed in the **Cahier du Sud**, were largely based upon Greek mythology.

Marguerite Yourcenar had been admired by a small group of faithful readers for twenty years before she came to the attention of the general public with **Mémoires d'Hadrien (Memoirs of Hadrian)** in 1951. The book is in the form of an imaginary letter written by the Emperor Hadrian—when near death—to his heir, Marcus Aurelius. His purpose is to add to Marcus' philosophical education the practical lessons that his own life, lived to the fullest, had offered him.

Marguerite Yourcenar had taken up and abandoned this work several times during the 1920's and the 1930's. In 1948 she received a trunk left with friends in Switzerland and filled with correspondence and other belongings from her pre-war years. Among many letters, she came across one that began "My dear Marc." She wondered to what forgotten friend or lover it had been written. With a shock she realized that it was Marcus Aurelius, and that the letter was the beginning of her latest attempt to write the book. From that moment on, she knew she had to finish it "whatever the cost." In previous attempts she had puzzled over the viewpoint to adopt for the novel. Now, after living through a decade of trauma and disorder in world affairs, she saw clearly that Hadrian should be considered primarily as the good prince.

Although, in trying to recreate history from within, with all exactitude of which she was capable, Marguerite Yourcenar believed that she was narrowing the audience who would read the book; **Hadrian** was an immediate and enormous success. In a world where the great task was binding up the wounds left by war,people sympathized with the great emperor--a humanist, a lover of all that was Greek, a man who could reconcile differing viewpoints, who felt responsible for the beauty of the world around him, and who was firmly resolved to be useful. They recognized him as being capable of loving and inspiring love, of drawing upon great strength, but also of succumbing to weakness, of succeeding as a prince and as a human being. Two of his best assets: the ability to establish a durable peace and to face the future squarely had, after the disruptions and uncertainties of World War II,an almost universal appeal.

Because the emperor had tried to neglect nothing that would enrich human life, the book shines with all the artistic and philosophic lights of the second century A.D. To write it, Marguerite Yourcenar did what she always does when embarking on any subject: she did her research thoroughly. In this case, she reconstructed Hadrian's library, immersed herself in everything that he had read or written, traveled the roads that he had traveled, and looked at or handled objects that he had loved.

Memoirs of Hadrian is not just an historical novel, as certain critics would have it. In an attempt to define her role in the creation of this work, Marguerite Yourcenar describes herself as an "historian-poet and novelist."Her research extended to the most minute details. Carlo Bronne told the story in his speech welcoming her into membership in the Royal Belgian Academy of French Language and Literature,of a learned critic who rebuked the author for telling about a woman piling up sesterces. Since they were convex, he claimed, the scene was impossible. "Wrong!"--the writer knew exactly how many could be stacked up without their falling, since she had experimented with them first. She must have enjoyed that moment, because she does not like pretentious people.2 This attention to detail, invaluable to an historian, is not enough

2. Marguerite Yourcenar, **Discours de réception à l'Académie royale belge de langue et de littérature française** (Paris: Gallimard, 1971), pp. 15-16.

for a poet. To make the Emperor live again, the author adapted methods evolved by Ignatius Loyola and the Hindu ascetics. That is, she looked at the second century with the soul of a second-century person. She says that she actually saw the people and events with an inner vision and participated with them through what she calls "sympathetic magic."3 Finally it is the novelists's role to find the form necessary and to shape the work.

Besides **Hadrian,** her most widely read and translated work is **L'Oeuvre au noir** **(The Abyss)** (1968). Like **Hadrian,** it was begun in the 1920's. At that time it was a part of a roman-fleuve, or, as she later referred to it, a "roman-ocean," the ambitious project of her first years as a writer.4 It appearred, in embryonic form, as one of three short stories in **La Mort conduit l'attelage** 'Death Drives the Team,' in 1934.

The main characters in these novels--Hadrian and Zeno--share some points of view. Their attitude toward women, self-discipline, and their need to investigate and learn everything that might help to explain the human condition, are similar. They also have in common a certain taste for magic and hermetic rites and for philosophy. If they have similarities, however, their situations and their backgrounds are entirely different. Hadrian reigned in the second century A.D. The world of that time seems to us to be stable and less complex; the problems easy to see, in part because of the distance that separates us from them, in part too because history cannot supply us with all of the details. Zeno, on the other hand, who lived in the sixteenth century, belongs to a world in turmoil, much like our own. Unlike Hadrian, he was without influence and was persecuted by those in

---

3. "Carnets de Notes de **Mémoires d'Hadrien**" ("Reflections on the Composition of **Memoirs of Hadrian**") in **Oeuvres romanesques** (Paris: Gallimard, 1982), p. 526; E 328-29.

4. **Souvenirs pieux** (Monaco: Editions Alphée, 1973), p, 241 .

8

power. The tone of **L'Oeuvre au noir** is a great deal more somber than that of **Mémoires d'Hadrien.** This is due in some measure to the temperaments of the protagonists and to the periods described in the novels. More importantly, however, it is due to the times during which Marguerite Yourcenar wrote them. Around 1950 it was believed that people of good will could come to an agreement that would result in world peace; by 1968 pessimism had taken hold of both the author and her readers.

The French title, **L'Oeuvre au noir,** litterally means "the black work" and refers to the first step in the magnum opus of the alchemists. Zeno, himself an alchemist, is also a cleric, a physician, and, above all, a philosopher. Here we have all of the essential ingredients for the exciting and dangerous experiments by which novelty is distilled. In this work, as in **Hadrian,** both a man, (fictitious this time) and his era are portrayed. The Renaissance princes and the great patrician families live vividly in this novel, as do the farmers who are slaves to their little plot of land, and the workers who are caught between owners, machines, and lay-offs. There are also religious people, some of them devoted to God, and not just to the Church. Among these is the Prior of the Franciscans, a mystic--as is Zeno at times--and one of the very few saints in Yourcenar's works.

Catholics, Anabaptists,clerics and the laity, almost all are ready, insofar as they are able, to persecute those who happen to differ with them. Learned men have their place, alongside those who are merely erudite. There are the searchers and the self-satisfied. Among them move two men, a soldier and a scholar, named Henry Maximilian and Zeno. Filled with a humanistic philosophy which is insufficient to sustain them in the face of the ill-will that they meet, they set out at the beginning of the novel to "take a tour of their prison." The two, for different reasons, are caught in a trap that, at first, they did not even see. This trap is what Marguerite Yourcenar calls the world's labyrinth in the title of her next major work.

Madame Yourcenar has said that the virtues she most admires are intelligence, simplicity, kindness, and justice. She both judges and acts on these principles. More and more she has concentrated on such basic human responses. She has simplified her way of life. Her tastes in the visual arts tend toward those which portray things in their natural simplicity, such

as the work of the old Chinese masters and some un-
named photographers. In literature, she favors a sim-
pler, less ornate style. Life on Mount Desert Island
has led her into what might be called her "geolologi-
cal period," when time and events are measured by the
mountains and the ocean's waves. For her, the universe is one, and she feels a kinship not only with
other people, but with trees, animals, the whole world
of nature. Any narrowness, be it on the basis of country, sex, age, or creed is foreign to her. She still
travels to see new things or renew her contact with
those she knows. She has become increasingly involved
with groups to promote social justice, civil rights,
and conservation, and with those established to protect wildlife and the quality of life. She has said
that she has many things still to do, the most important of which is not, perhaps, the writing of books.

Note on Alexis

While other works had been privately printed, **Alexis** (1929) is the first work that Marguerite Yourcenar had accepted for publication. The subject of the novel is the search on the part of a very sensitive and talented young man for the freedom to react to the world and to express himself in the most authentic way possible without the need for pretense or lies. Alexis, the protagonist, is a bisexual. To create his portrait and to develop the atmosphere and story line of the novel, Yourcenar drew upon the life stories of two different men. From the elder came the setting-- Eastern Europe of the pre-World War I era--and the plot. The other, younger by almost a generation, served as a model for Alexis' personality traits. The authenticity of this fictional voice has been reaffirmed by letters from numerous readers. For Alexis' beginnings as an artist--his struggle to find his own particular subject and ways in which to express it-- the author no doubt made use of her own search at the time for reaching these same goals.

The theme of bisexuality has led, inevitably, to comparisons between this novel and the works of Andre Gide. Yourcenar found the title in Vergil's "Second Eclogue" where Gide found **Corydon.**It is also true that the sub-title of **Alexis, Traité d'un vain combat** 'Account of a Futile Struggle' echoes **Corydon's Traité d'un vain désir.** Yet Yourcenar insists that it was not Gide, but rather Rainer-Maria Rilke who influenced **Alexis.** It was his scruples, his religiosity, and his feelings of tenderness toward all of his fellow-creatures, which Yourcenar admired in Rilke's **Notebooks of Malte Laurids Brigge** and his **Duino Elegies,** that are reflected in **Alexis.**

Bisexuality is an important theme in this and later works of Marguerite Yourcenar, in particular **Hadrien** and **L'Oeuvre au noir.** Some critics have stressed Yourcenar's propensity for male characters to the virtual exclusion of women--a view now gradually being modified--and have often overemphasized her interest in homosexuality. They have neglected to consider this theme in relation to the fabric of her work.

Creating the tone of **Alexis** was one of the most difficult artistic questions that the author had to face. Aiming to avoid both prudishness and obscenity, she settled upon the sober style traditionally adopted for sermons and for the "examination of conscience," i.e. a choice of language that probes nuances of feeling while maintaining the decorum suitable for addressing Alexis' young wife.

Most of the critical emphasis has been on the theme of homosexuality or on the diction of this novel. We have chosen instead to comment on it as the best representation of one of Marguerite Yourcenar's primary images: the house.

Alexis has appeared in ten editions between 1929 and 1982, one of which, in 1971, was a limited edition text with an original print signed by Salvador Dali. The novel has been translated into nine languages to date, of which English is not one.

The House: Image and Reality in **Alexis**

Alexis, ou le Traité d'un vain combat, is the story of a very young man written by a very young author --both are 25 at its close.[1] Concerned primarily with the problem of individual freedom and responsibility, this is a novel about leaving home. It is not surprising, then, to find that the dominating image of the house is one of its principal forces.

In this novel, written in the form of a letter and intended to show how and why he is different--the word "homosexuality" is never mentioned--Alexis tells Monique, the wife he has left, his life story, because he believes that the present is determined by the past.

Alexis is a psychological novel in which the main character struggles to analyze and interpret his actions and the motives behind them. He promises at the outset to be as accurate and as sincere as he can, and indeed his voice often hesitates as he corrects a word, clarifies a statement, criticizes his own efforts at explanation, or seeks a truer or more general foundation for his thought. The tension created by the search for the right tone, one that will express every nuance of his character and guarantee the reader's understanding; by the recognition, at every step, that such basic truths can never be expressed perfectly in the same words that must fit everyone; and by the struggle between his instincts and his conscience; is one of the outstanding characteristics of this novel.

Even though convinced of Alexis' good will, the reader is still aware that in this, as in any story told in the first person, there will be a gap between statement and truth due to the narrator's own difficulty in understanding himself completely or in admitting what he may feel. Among the touchstones provided by the author to help us judge the protagonist's reactions, one of the most important is the house.

---

1. Paris: Au Sans Pareil, 1929; rpt. **Oeuvres romanesques,** Bibliothèque de la Pléiade (Paris:Gallimard, 1982). All references to novels are to the Pléiade edition.

Among the traditional associations evoked by this image, which nearly always carries positive valorization, we find here the identification with the body, the mother, and the family.It is also a symbol of refuge and of continuity with the past. Alexis' overt response to Woroïno, his birthplace and childhood home, is straightforward: "I was very fond of it" (Pl 13), and he acknowledges its importance by beginning his explanations there. His descriptions of life in the house are not, however, merely undifferenciated affirmations of its eternal values. It is especially at those times when Woroino's characteristics seem different from, even the antithesis of, those of the oneiric house to which literate readers respond automatically, that we can expect to find details revelatory of Alexis' make-up.

Descriptions of a home commonly begin with the physical traits of the house itself.It is significant, then, to note that Alexis introduces other elements first: water, ghosts, and silence.

Trying to discover the clues in his youth-- "that ignorance that we call peace"-- to his present personality, Alexis has often "bent over this past" (Pl 11). As Gaston Bachelard has pointed out, the image of leaning over the past immediately summons up the image of deep waters.2 It is therefore natural that Woroïno's ponds are the first of its features to be named. As a child, Alexis was afraid of them. Monique once described them as "great pieces of gray sky that had fallen to earth and that were trying to rise up again in the form of mist" (Pl 11).

This depressing and disturbing image serves to alert the reader to the general tone of the house. It is colorless, sad, and heavy. The water's mirror can reflect only dimly and cannot perform the idealizing function of clear water. The lack of movement and of sound is a foreboding of death. Not being able to see into the depths of the water, Alexis cannot penetrate its secret, and this also worries him. He concludes that peace, like silence, is only a surface and that his childhood was, in fact, only "great peace on the

---

2. **L'Eau et les rêves** (Paris: José Corti, 1942), p. 74.

edge of great anxiety" (Pl 11). These ponds, then, are a material presence whose qualities dominate the house and its inhabitants. The words **triste** 'sad' and **morne** 'dismal' will be used over and over to describe every aspect of life there.

Ghosts, whose real or threatened presence is a characteristic of a very old house, inhabit Woroino. Alexis and his immediate family are the last of a lineage (Pl 13) and less alive than their ancestors, whose images the mirrors reflect (Pl 13). Their lives are pale reflections of the life once lived in the house. The living, as well as the dead, are ghosts.

Woroïno is permeated with silence, which Alexis later perceives as "congealed matter," one that becomes progressively harder and is difficult to remove, with life continuing only beneath it (Pl 16). This suggests an ice image, especially since the house is also described as seeming "fragile" in a white snow setting (Pl 14). These brittle, cold images are far from the cozy warmth proper to the oneiric house. Yet its fragile appearance is deceptive. Alexis recognizes that the house is in fact more durable than the individuals who inhabit it and may even outlast the family line. Strangely, although Alexis is attached to the house, he sees it as indifferent to people, living out its own life which people do not understand.

Silence is not merely a characteristic; it is a rule. There is no joy here, or any other strongly expressed emotion. Laughter and tears are both suppressed. Every conversation is carried on in low tones, so as not to awaken memories that would be better left asleep (Pl 13-14).

Alexis goes on to depict Woroïno as white with many windows and columns in the French style popular during the rule of Catherine the Great. It was built for parties, as a display of wealth, with rooms large enough to provide good acoustics for music and to accommodate many guests for parties. But it is too late for the reader to be convinced by these convivial images. He responds immediately to the idea that the Géra family, merely dim reflections of the dead, **are** the guests (Pl 14), and guests who are not fitted to the house's functions.

All of the elements of this description contribute to creating a house of the dead: water that does not reflect clearly; mirrors that reflect only ghosts; empty rooms; movement that has slowed from the lively parties of another age to the monotonous life of Alexis' present; and especially the silence to which all sounds are reduced, and which "seemed always to be growing greater" (Pl 16) as the imaginary gradually dominates the real. All of this makes of Woroïno a mausoleum, the last house that any family will occupy.

The house is more than the real scene of a dreamer's childhood; it stands as an embodiment of a past: that of the dreamer and of his family. In terms of classical psychology, it functions in the role of the superego, imposing the family's value system and its lifestyle.

Alexis' way of looking at life has been shaped by this house since he was a child. It is the visible sign that he belongs to one of those old families in Bohemia that cannot change because no one notices what they are, only what they were. The Géras are respected in their region because of "a certain field marshall" whose exact dates no one remembers (Pl 13). A vague past, as Bachelard says,[3] symbolizes a search for the self, and it is this search, certainly, that comprises the story line of this novel. As a child Alexis becomes accustomed to relative poverty but also to the realization that he is expected to behave in such a way as to maintain the family honor.

He feels that to try to reach the same importance his ancestors had would be somehow presumptuous, but still he fears that his sexual preferences, which set him apart from other men, will be neither understood nor accepted, that the family status will be diminished by his being different.

His family goes on living, he says, out of a sense of "loyalty...to the house, I guess, to my ancestors, too" (Pl 12). In the course of the novel he will work toward setting up his own values, establishing a lifestyle that is his alone. Nevertheless, his marriage and his begetting a son are interpreted as responses to "a blind sense of duty" to the family (Pl 71) and,

---

3. **La Terre et les rêveries du repos** (Paris: José Corti, 1948) p. 124.

when Daniel is born, one of Alexis' first reactions is to see the ancestral portraits as no longer projecting their will, " [they] stopped being a real presence and became merely an apparition" (Pl 71). He has fulfilled his obligation to the race.

The idea of the house as representative of the past can allow a child an early sense of history and provide valuable guides for structuring his value system and his first attempts to define himself. This positive value, however, is rendered negative by Alexis' belief, when still a child, that the past is more important than the present (Pl 12). Such a conviction leaves the living with no role to fill except to provide a successor before they die and become part of this past. Alexis, a timid and fearful child, is slow in developing a strong sense of his intrinsic worth and sees independence primarily as a negative rather than as a positive goal.

Both Alexis' thoughts on the past and his feeling that the living are only shades of the dead, a theme that will be even further developed in **La Nouvelle Eurydice** 'The New Eurydice,'4 are made concrete in the image of his mirror which was "a little cloudy," and gave only a dim reflection of himself.This mirror represents, in the interior of the house, the gray ponds outside. The material sadness "redoubles [his] agony" (Pl 33).

The house, for Alexis, is also, as is normal, a maternal image. His father is an authoritarian, not merely an authority, figure. The child identifies with his mother and sisters, because he shares with them their fear of the other male members of the household. The house has, in common with the women, the silence and calm that Alexis associates with femininity. His mother and sisters, though, are more than calm: their faces are described as "obliterated" (Pl 21), another description apt for ghosts. The next sentence mentions their premature deaths. Monique, by contrast, is filled with life, "wonderful vitality" (Pl 64). She will not be subjugated by the house as the others have been.

---

4. Paris: Grasset, 1931.

Alexis' first attempts to discover himself at Wo-roïno are expressed both symbolically and overtly with references to the house. One of his early memories is of a painting showing a musician surrounded by an attentive audience that gives the impression of having received an important revelation. Identification with the central figure in this tableau is both appealing and terrifying to a boy so young that he has not as yet received any revelations himself (Pl 16). Even more significant to the reader is the placement of the painting. It hangs in the corridor leading to his bedroom. The corridor is traditionally symbolic of the search for the self, while one's own room represents the inner self. This special place of recollection is of particular importance to a child who not only experiences, but needs, solitude. Alexis does indeed decide to become a musician and takes as his goal the translation of the "special quality of the silence that [he] never found anywhere but at Woroïno"(Pl 12).

The solitude and silence--both of which are potentially positive values--contribute for Alexis to the image of the house as refuge. Not only the dreamer's "cell" inside, but the larger unit of the house with its gardens is enclosed. The fence that separates Wo-roïno from the road--which represents the world--stands as an ambiguous image. It is futile no doubt to ask whether it is primarily a means of keeping the Géras in, or other people out. Almost certainly, it is, in turn, both. As a child, Alexis used to put his hands through the bars of this fence to give flowers --a symbol of the beauty that is so important to him --to the small gypsy children as they passed by. Later, the house will seem not a refuge but a prison.

The negative values of these same two qualities are also present, however, because, contrary to the characteristics of the oneiric house, Woroïno is seen by Alexis as always too large for the family, and always cold (Pl 14).

At fifteen, he is sent away to boarding school in Pressburg. Inevitably his reactions to his home are either reinforced or changed by his acquiring a different frame of reference and perspective on it. The school is described as entirely gray, unrelieved by white as at Woroïno, and crowded, for he has no room to himself, but only a bed in a "dismal line-up of beds" (Pl 25). Instead of the silence and solitude of hidden secrets dimly perceived as being under the surface of the ponds, Alexis discovers in communal living

18

an exposure that he finds even more frightening. The gray walls of the school shut him in with a group of other adolescent boys whom he finds brutal, shocking, and cynical. The women whom he encounters in the boys' conversations or on excursions out of the school are repugnant to him, and he responds with hate toward those not worthy of his respect (Pl 25). Instead of the surface innocence and purity of his early childhood, disturbing hints of his "forbidden inclinations" begin to appear, and the first result of these tendencies is to "hem us in within ourselves" (Pl 35).

This intolerance and rigidity typical of children is, in Alexis' case, aggravated by a fastidiousness, both physical and moral, that is very much a part of his character. He suffers from the depressing atmosphere and overly close contact with his schoolmates. The search for moral purity is revealed by his habit of the examination of conscience and by the scruples that both reassure and terrify him. Deprived of music and of solitude, unable to tolerate the "soiled surroundings" at Pressburg (Pl 28), and ill from the mental and physical strain of coping with these problems, Alexis begs to return to Woroïno.

The return to one's country, or to one's home, is viewed as the psychological equivalent of the return to the mother. It is to his mother that he writes asking to come home. She is the one who comes to get him and bring him back into the world.

Alexis has been unable to find his place in the all-male community at Pressburg, and, once home, he likewise rejects the company and the occupations of the male members of the family. He still feels really at home only in the feminine atmosphere of the house, as opposed to the estate administered by his brothers. The reader knows that this choice is permanent because Alexis says of those outside affairs "it was more than I was doing, more than I would ever do..." (Pl 30). He is thus already determined never to fill a traditional male role himself, even though he begins vaguely to understand that it, too, has its place.

His relief at reaching the safe refuge that Woroïno represents for him is greater than outward circumstances seem to warrant: "I felt as though I were saved" (Pl 30). It is from himself that he feels saved, by being protected from the outside contacts that encourage the development of those tendencies that he himself so rigorously condemns.

19

Although he is once again part of the family, accepting without serious question its "rather dismal
morality" (Pl 30) and the role within it that he believes he cannot change (Pl 35), he is at the same
time alienated from the other members. He is separated by his inability to talk about what preoccupies
him, by his feelings of being different, and by the
solitude that he needs. This isolation is shown by a
reference to the house in which he has been"**relegated**"
to a distant wing" (Pl 29, emphasis ours).

Staying a Woroïno, he begins to develop, between
the ages of sixteen and nineteen, the music that is to
be his. He wishes to express that distinctive silence
of Woroino, made up of words not said aloud and filled
with sadness (Pl 15-16). Music has another quality
that appeals to Alexis: it is discreet. It can mourn
without saying why (Pl 16).

Such discretion is essential to Alexis, because it
is also at this stage that he "discovers beauty" (Pl
31). Having become "reasonable" (Pl 30), he leaves
the house only in broad daylight on fine days, but the
avoidance of night and darkness does not keep him from
succumbing to his own nature, which does not change
with external factors, natural or imaginary.

When Alexis has made Woroïno part of his music,the
actual house is less necessary to him, and he begins
to see it less as a refuge than as a prison. He feels
oppressed by his older brothers and fears further opportunities to indulge in what he views as illicit relationships. Imagining that he will be freer elsewhere, he presses his mother to allow him to leave
home and to continue his musical career in Vienna. In
a symbolic gesture on the eve of his departure, he
opens his window and watches people going by on the
road, singing. Although they are on the other side of
the fence, he feels closer to them, knowing that the
next day he will open the gates and leave Woroïno.
Identifying the house with himself, he says, "Leaving
[it], it seems easier to leave ourselves" (Pl 36).

In the next three years Alexis passes through several stages of emotional development and lives in a
series of temporary homes. On his arrival in Vienna,
he makes up his mind to renounce his leanings, which
he holds to be "guilty" (Pl 39). He is surrounded,
though, by people from whom he has previously been

protected. Such contacts are "sordid;" the women he
meets do nothing to improve his opinion of them (Pl
40). The rented rooms in Vienna are a shock to him
after Woroino. He suffers both from the wretchedness
of the house and the contact with the people he meets
there. His room repels him. It is sad and dirty; and
its false elegance wrings his heart (Pl 40). His fas-
tidious nature is, at first, offended by other people's
having lived in it before, but gradually he begins to
visualize them, and they become the familiar ghosts of
his new home.

As he comes to know himself better, he finds that
enforced virtue can last only a certain length of time
before he succumbs to temptation again. Whereas at
Woroino he feared occasions for backsliding, it is now
his own body that he fears;and, since he believes that
his instincts are communicated to his soul, there is
no longer any asylum (Pl 45).

The solitude he experiences in Vienna is different
from that at Woroino since he cannot seek out a sympathetic person at will. The mirror, not dim as at Woroino, "inflicts" his own presence on him and becomes an
object of hatred. Two other images of the offensive
nature of reality follow immediately. Evening shadows
fall on his room like "an additional layer of grime,"
and the noise from the open window, the insistent presence of others, tires him until he cannot think. It is
then that he has to leave the room, his temporary
refuge, in search of the pleasure that will necessar-
ily entail humiliation upon his defeat (Pl 46). Since
there is no fence here, he feels a prisoner of his instincts (Pl 42) and later of his self (Pl 46), seen
objectively as a separate entity. Images of the prison
are only interior during this period.

Remorse tempts him to forget his past, but since
he is renouncing the present and the future by vowing
not to give in to his inclinations, he clings to his
memories. His dreams will not allow him to forget: "I
realized the danger in stagnant waters" (Pl 47). The
same water, present at Woroino, tempts him in Vienna.
He sees it as impure, and his thoughts turn to suicide.

After a serious illness, he is invited to Wand, the
summer home of some distant relatives, the Prince and
Princess of Mainau, for recuperation. This place gives
the same impression "of great age and peaceful continuation" as Woroïno, and Alexis feels so at home that he

21

almost forgets the harsh realities of the city(Pl 54).
Life becomes a sort of midsummer night's dream(Pl 55).
55). Here he can at least imagine happiness, if not
experience it.

In this atmosphere Alexis becomes like a child
again, allowing others to make decisions for him.
Even his fears about himself are lulled in the absence
of temptation. In this unreal situation he meets and
marries Monique, desperately reaching for goals that
he knows the family approves.

For more than a year after his marriage Alexis
does not have a home, at least not one where he even
partially belongs. The hotel rooms on their honeymoon
he describes as cold and bare, reflecting the lack of
warmth and the unfamiliarity in his marriage. There
is no solitude, but no intimacy either to compensate
for it (Pl 65). Their windows are opened "futilely"
(Pl 65) on the warm Italian evenings, because Alexis
is afraid of countries "where happiness is in the
flesh" (P. 62).

When the marriage is finally consumated, Alexis
views Monique's gift of herself as maternal and thinks
of himself as her first child. He imagines that every
man is really looking for another mother in his wife
(Pl 63).

Alexis has completely given up music since he
feels it belongs to another world, one which he is resigned to having left forever. To him music has always
been associated with an opening of opportunities. Enclosed in his marriage, Alexis' music, part of "[his]
dream life" becomes "dried up" or "frozen" within him
(Pl 66).The couple's first home in Vienna is no better; it tires and bores him. Because Alexis feels cut
off from his former life, he looks with disfavor on
the furnishings, chosen entirely by Monique, that hold
no memories and the mirrors that know neither him nor
his wife. Without his music and without the freedom
of his former life, he sees in their new home only
barren rooms where they will be imprisoned (Pl 67).

Monique feels it appropriate, however, that Woroino be the scene of the birth of their first child.She
has had it restored at her own expense. When they arrive, Alexis finds it little changed, although it does
seem even larger than before (Pl 69). In other words,
it still exerts the same power over him. Just as marriage has imposed outward changes in his way of life,

so has the family home undergone superficial modifica-
tion. Neither has changed fundamentally.

In this milieu Alexis feels it even more natural
to be a child, and casts Monique in the role of moth-
er--his own or merely the Mother. As she lies in the
huge ceremonial bed with its heavy curtains, in a dark
room, he almost expects her to give him her blessing
as his mother used to do. But he thinks also of the
generations of women who awaited their child's birth
or their own death in the same bed. The series of
images convey darkness and enclosure, associated with
the bed where Monique will give birth, are an obvious
representation of an infant's first home.

This place belongs to Monique and Daniel. Just as
he once rejected the men's work outside, Alexis now
refuses to stay near the master bedroom, thus symbolically rejecting the roles of husband and head of a
household. He chooses instead to retreat to the room
in the distant wing that he had as a boy and to his
former bed which knows the curves of his body and allows him to dream his sixteen-year-old dreams. In this
way he rejoins his past and is reunited with himself
(Pl 72). His behavior reminds us of Alexis' earlier
reflection that his son, Daniel, will continue the
line, and Alexis is free to go: "to die, or else to
begin to live again" (Pl 72).

On the last night at Woroïno--he and Monique were
to leave for Vienna after the summer season--Alexis
rediscovers his music. His entire soul has been reduced to one monotonous melody, and his life is made
up of silence (Pl 74). Fortified by his boyhood
dreams, he wants to be free, to live by and for his
art, and to express himself completely. As before, the
refuge has become a prison, and Alexis sees his hands
as instruments capable of opening its doors. His only
regret, for which he asks forgiveness in the closing
of the novel, is not that he left Monique, but that he
stayed so long.

Alexis leaves home for the third time, more experienced, it is true, and understanding himself somewhat better. But on several occasions during his story
we have seen that when he is in a familiar home situation, life outside tends to seem to him only a short
interlude, easily forgotten (Pl 30 and 55). On the
other hand, when he has been too deeply touched by
what seems to him sordid reality, he clings to his

23

memories and to his past (Pl 47). While he has his
music and feels strong, he can carry Woroïno with him.
When, for whatever reason, he loses his inspiration,
he needs to come home again.

The house is a vital image not only in **Alexis**, but
throughout Marguerite Yourcenar's work. In **La Nouvelle
Eurydice** Vivombre is,as its name implies, an even more
ambiguous home-tomb image. It, too, stands as the living presence of the characters' life and past. The
house as an image identifiable with the human body is
most clearly expressed in **Feux** when Clytemnestra says
of Agamemnon "he just left me standing like a big deserted house" (Pl 1116; E 103). A striking example of
the house as a reflection of a family's lifestyle and
values is Forestel in **L'Oeuvre au noir.** The minute description of its decoration and furnishings is,in itself, a negative commentary on the materialistic and
acquisitive couple inhabiting it and provides a clue
to the author's attitude toward them (Pl 1805 ff; E
320 ff). Chenonceaux, in the essay "Ah, mon beau château"'Ah, My Lovely Château' included in **Sous Bénéfice
d'inventaire** 'With Reservations'5 and the houses in
Le Labyrinthe du monde 6 retain and reflect the political, artistic, and personal history of generations
of people of all classes whose lives were centered
there, as well as the animals and the elements that
complete the surroundings.

Yet the two principal houses in Madame Yourcenar's
work, besides Woroino, must be considered to be Gemara
in **Denier du rêve** and Kratovitsy in **Coup de grâce.**
Gemara embodies the spirit of a family, and its image
is capable of sustaining that spirit in Rosalia, who
commits suicide rather than lose it, and in Don Ruggero, her mad father, whose life goes on in distant
Gemara rather than in the crude reality of his asylum.
Kratovitsy's image is as haunting as the troubled

---

5. Paris: Gallimard, 1962, pp. 56-115.

6. **Souvenirs pieux** (Paris: Gallimard, 1974) and **Archives du Nord** (Paris: Gallimard, 1977).

lives of its people. As well as being a tale of unre-
ciprocated love and violent death, **Coup de grâce** is a
story that traces the gradual destruction of a house,
and with it the crumbling of a country and a way of
life.

The house, wherever it appears in Marguerite Yourcenar's work, is a physical manifestation of the spirit of an individual or of a family. Well managed and
inhabited by good people, it is an island or refuge
from the dangers and repressions of society as a
whole. Far too easily, however, it becomes a focus
for ostentation, an excuse for not considering anyone
who does not belong there, and a concentrated influence which limits not only its members' freedom to develop as individuals, but even their desire to do so.

In **Alexis** the house is alternately an extension of
the man: another self, another mother, the nearest approximation to the primordial refuge,and a reminder of
his inadequacies: the glory of a past he cannot emu-
late, the social obligations he feels unable to fulfill, the differences between himself and others that
prevent an easy access to a well-defined role in life.

His home is the visible proof, if we doubt his own
estimate, that Alexis has always been cut off from the
society around him and apart even within the house and
therefore within the family. It is the embodiment of
a sadness he cannot dispel, of a space he cannot fill.
He wages his"futile struggle" to be so completely master of himself that he can change to fulfill his own
expectations, but succeeds no better in that than he
does in becoming master of the house at Woroïno. In
the end he decides to accept the life that his instincts dictate and his musician's hands allow. He
will express his personal conception of Woroïno in his
music. To do so, however, he must give up the role
in family and society that Woroïno, as his ancestral
home, also represents. He needs to live according to
his own values, but he needs to be cradled and direc-
ted by a mother-figure. These conflicts, alternately
aggravated and assuaged by Alexis' contacts with the
house are, at several points,temporarily resolved. His
ambivalent feelings toward Woroïno reflect his ambivalent feelings toward himself.One cannot be sure whether his victory--or his defeat--will be definitive.

Note on **Denier du rêve**

As Marguerite Yourcenar became familiar, through her travels, with the Italian people, especially those in the country and the working class sections of the city, she began to try to communicate in her works an Italian tone, reminiscent of the baroque opera.

Besides those characters in **Denier du rêve** who had real-life counterparts, there are others who are composites of many people whom the author observed or whose stories were elaborated from small news items in the daily newspaper. Their milieu is drawn from the neighborhood in Rome where Marguerite Yourcenar herself was living and from the historical city, familiar to her from research for early versions of Hadrian's story.

The writing of the first version of this novel, in 1933, presented many technical problems. The difficulties of furnishing a comprehensive slice-of-life of a people and a time were complicated by her trying to incorporate into this fabric the myths and dreams that were primary concerns for her during this period. The result was a text encumbered by too many allusions and written on too many levels.

In contrast to the unadorned language of **Alexis,** lyrical and highly realistic passages are juxtaposed in **Denier du rêve.** Although the book was well received by the majority of its critics and readers in the 1930's, with the exception of those who objected to the author's liberal political views, it was not widely read, and Marguerite Yourcenar herself remained dissatisfied with it.

In 1959, therefore, she undertook a complete recasting of the book, and in 1961 she again rewrote it, this time in play form, upon the request of a theater director. The dramatic version, "Rendre à César" 'Render unto Caesar' appears in **Théâtre I** (1971).

The people who inhabit this fictional world have remained very much alive for their author. Sixty years have passed since she saw the first models she would use, but they have grown and developed in the process of reworking the novel. Interestingly, some, like Father Cicca, did not find their real voice until "Rendre à César." Yet even with these definitive versions published, the characters have not told their whole story. The Registry printed at the end of the play shows that they each have specific dates and places of birth and death, outside the time-frame of the novel and play. One of the author's projects for the future is a volume of sequels in which will appear some of these characters' lives subsequent to the novel, as they are already known to Marguerite Yourcenar.

Little has so far been written on this volume, whose rich imagery merits a series of studies devoted to it. The following essay attempts to begin this work.

There have been six editions of **Denier du rêve**, the first in 1934, the major revision in 1959. The novel has been translated into five languages. In English (1982) it is entitled **A Coin in Nine Hands.**

Mirrors and Masks in **Denier du rêve**

According to its author, **Denier du rêve** is among the first French novels to reveal "the holow reality behind the bloated facade of fascism."[1] Set in Rome of 1933, Year XI of the fascist rule of the dictator, referred to here simply as "Caesar," the novel depicts the lives of a group of people in public, but more often in private; their interactions, but more often their solitude; their successes and their hopes, but more often their failure and their despair. We are given the telling details that make each of the characters' lives unique, but we are also shown what the author calls their **quid divinum**. This is done, in large measure, by complex mirror effects by means of which the reader sees each character as he presents himself (his mask), perceives himself (his inner reality), is viewed by others (his outer reality), and himself serves as a mirror reflecting those around him.

The human problems of each man's intrinsic lonliness, his search for understanding from another human being, the struggle against oppression or limitations and the search for a truth beyond daily existence will be familiar to readers of **Mémoires d'Hadrien** and **L'Oeuvre au noir.**[2] There are two principal differences that should be noted. First, **Denier du rêve** was originally written during the period when the author was

---

1. Paris: Grasset, 1934; rpt. in **Oeuvres romanesques** (Paris: Gallimard,1982). All references to novels, unless otherwise marked, will be to this Pléiade edition. **A Coin in Nine Hands**. trans. Dori Katz in colaboration with the author(New York: Farrar, Straus, and Giroux, 1982).

2. Paris: Plon,1951 and Paris: Gallimard, 1968. Both rpt. in the Pléiade edition, 1982. **Memoirs of Hadrian,** trans. Grace Frick in collaboration with the author (1954; rpt. New York: Farrar, Straus and company, 1963) and **The Abyss,** trans. Grace Frick in collaboration with the author (New York: Farrar, Straus, and Giroux, 1976).

particularly concerned with the interrelationship of dreams and myths with reality as it is commonly conceived. Secondly, Hadrian and Zeno are both introspective and eminently capable of self-analysis. They are, therefore, less in need of mirrors or masks than are the more ordinary characters in **Denier du rêve.**

It is not surprising that a novel which seeks to integrate the worlds of dream and reality should be pervaded by the mirror--that profoundly ambivalent image which both reflects the real world and serves as a door to a magic one beyond. While certainly not an unusual image in literature, mirrors are of particular interest to readers of **Denier du rêve** first because of their number (the examples in this short study represent only a fraction of the total), and secondly because of their diversity. The characters in this novel too are provided with mirrors made to their measure. In the same way, Zeno found a mirror suited to different stages of his development: first, a multifaceted Florentine mirror in which he saw twenty Zenos imprisoned in their looking-glass world ends the section on his travels; and later, during his period of study and change, a magnifying glass reflects his own eye which he does not at first recognize. (Pl 670,705; E 145, 192). The looking-glass (or fountain) underlies many different types of reflections; each personality consults the sort of mirror in which he believes. Nor is it strange that the characters,originally conceived as members of a modern Roman commedia or tragedia dell'arte, should wear masks, which provide a surface, as mirrors do, but one which conceals rather than reveals.

An examination of the nature of the mirror images will illustrate their function with respect to the persons or things reflected in them, in order to arrive at a complete understanding of the view of life--its reality and its dreams, its statements and its poetry--that **Denier** seeks to convey. We shall also, but secondarily, consider the mask and how its functions are both integrated with and opposed to those of the mirror.

Passed from hand to hand, the coin itself serves as a tangible bond among the characters; it is the coin that buys dreams, those voluntary illusions that are perhaps "the only thing in the world that does not deceive" (Pl 169; E 6). With these illusions, each buys a kind of mirror in which, like Narcissus, he can see himself as the center of a world created so as to complement him.

As we follow the progress of the coin, we are given our first glimpse of the major characters, each with his basic mask, in search of his most precious illusion. Paolo Farina (the naive provincial) first gives the coin to Lina Chiari (the good-hearted prostitute) to purchase the illusion of love, since his wife (Angiola) has left him. Lina, who has just discovered that she has cancer, pays Giulio Lovisi (the hard-working middle-class, hen-pecked merchant) for lipstick to create the illusion that she is still beautiful and healthy. Giulio buys five candles in church from Rosalia di Credo (the totally devoted daughter and sister) to obtain hope, i.e., the illusion that he can influence and improve his circumstances. Rosalia, who has lost her family and her raison d'etre, buys death, in the form of a plate of coals, to escape to her real home, Gemara, an idealized vision of her family place in Sicily. Marcella (the idealistic revolutionary) gets the coin from her and makes token payment for a revolver with which to assassinate the dictator, i.e.,to create the illusion of effective individual action. Her estranged husband, Alessandro Sarte (the famous physician and man-about-town) who gets the coin from Marcella, buys flowers to give the illusion of a real love to his momentary encounter with Angiola (the self-centered actress). Dida, the old flower seller (the practical, limited peasant) gives the coin, to buy herself the illusion of generosity, to Clement Roux (the famous painter) who throws it into the Trevi Fountain to buy a future that his age and illness deny him.It is gathered from there by a working man, Dida's son, Oreste Marinunzi (a pawn, moved by others) who buys wine, the mirror in which the most powerful and flattering of illusions may be seen.

Mirrors that reflect objective reality appear scattered throughout **Denier** and serve as a point of reference for other, figurative, mirrors. Vanna Stevo, for example,after discovering that her exiled husband, Carlo, has recanted, immediately checks her hand-mirror and applies make-up "like a woman about to go out to meet someone" (Pl 215; E 70). Angiola, after an intimate scene in a theater loge, does the same thing. This reaction indicates that both of these women, one who defines herself as her famous husband's wife, and the other, who is an actress, are primarily

31

concerned with appearances. These two mirrors serve not only the function of self-contemplation for characters little given to reflective thought, but also the function of calling for change. Someone who looks at himself wishes to be seen and prepares himself for it. In these instances, the change involves make-up, the equivalent of the mask for the modern theater. Giulio Lovisi understands this feminine need; he was a constant witness to the "poses aimed at love, like the stage gestures actresses endlessly rehearse...he ferreted out the arrogant ones who used make-up as one more form of defiance; the ones in love who used it to keep from losing someone; the shy or plain ones who used ointments to hide their faces" (Pl 177-78; E 18). Adjusting their masks, these women ask advice and reassurance of their mirrors.

Photographs, a fixed mirror image, are also used occasionally not only to reflect objective reality to the subject but to convey it to another. Clement Roux is taken aback (Pl 265; E 140) and Vanna is alarmed (Pl 208; E 60) when Massimo recognizes them, because they do not know that he has seen their photographs. They react as though someone has surprised them while they were looking in their mirror.

Eyes are traditionally perceived as mirrors. In the passage from **L'Oeuvre au noir** cited above, Zeno notices that in each of the twenty images of himself are two shining eyes that are themselves mirrors (Pl 670-71; E 145). Furthermore, Gaston Bachelard points out that the gaze of others easily becomes offensive, and the eye no longer contemplates, but observes. 3 When Alessandro arrives at Marcella's home shortly after she has learned of Carlo Stevo's recantation, she angrily accuses him of having come only to "observe the effect of this disaster on me" (Pl 216; E 72). Marcella is forced to abandon the mask of formality intended to hold Vanna at a distance when she sees her "stubborn, almost insulting look" (Pl 208; E 61). Between certain of the characters this gaze never penetrates the mask of convention or banality that each wears. Giulio and Rosalia, for example, do not exchange thoughts, but only the polite formulae that suffice among well-bred people (Pl 181; E 23). Neither sees the other as he is, but only his predictable

---

3. **L'eau et les rêves** (Paris: Corti, 1942), p. 43.

reactions. In other situations (as with Marcella and
Vanna (Pl 207-15; E 160-71) rapport is reduced to a
series of violent positive and negative reactions.such
relationships are no more fruitful than if each were
to consult a mirror to reassure himself that his mask
is in place. Each remains essentially alone.

Surface reflections are especially apparent in
cases where one person is little more than a reflection of someone not present. Alessandro finds some
measure of consolation and some revenge with Angiola
when Marcella will not agree to return to him. Paolo
Farina is first attracted to Lina Chiari because of
her surface resemblance to his wife, Angiola.

We perceive the meeting of Lina and Paolo differently, however, since they meet beside a fountain.
This natural water image that is Narcissus' mirror
reveals an inner reality which is also a primary function of the mirror. Lest the glass seem too artificial, Marguerite Yourcenar takes care to include this
basic image at significant points in the novel: at the
very beginning (Pl 169; E 5); again just before and
just after the central chapter (Pl 203,240; E 53,105);
and as the last major image before the concluding
chapter (Pl 272 ff; E 149 ff). Its significant positions in the structure of the novel suggest that the
traditional values of reflection in water, i.e., beauty, purity, innocence, freshness, and depth are to be
understood as pertaining to all of the other mirrors.

Mirrors, a long tradition holds, remember. They
contain within themselves not only the outward appearance, but the nature of what they have reflected. Marcella thinks of Alessandro's house and of the mirrors
that "know" her. Rosalia, on the other hand, is hurt
by the realization that Gemara's mirrors would not
"recognize" any of her family. Clearly, we are meant
to understand that part of Marcella is still in some
respects the same as when she lived as Alessandro's
wife, but that all of the di Credos have changed so
radically as to be different people.

The penetrating perceptions of other people are
commonly used as mirrors. It is through them that the
reader knows, for example, that Paolo Farina had the
soul of a Don Quixote in the body of a Sancho Panza
(Pl 201; E 51). Most of the characters in this book
care a great deal about the impression that they make
on others. Their actions are, to varying degrees,

designed to elicit favorable reactions in those around
them. The strongest personalities are, predictably,the
least dependent on this confirming response. Marcella
is not to be deterred by opinion, although she does
weaken momentarily, tempted, first by the love and
peaceful existence that Alessandro offers and, secondly, by her half-maternal feelings for Massimo. Mother
Dida, in her monologue (Pl 250 ff; E 119 ff) notes and
refutes many adverse opinions of herself, but the only
one that moves her to action is the opinion of Father
Cicca whose eye is, for her, equivalent to the eye of
God, and then only when death (i.e., Marcella's assassination attempt) has passed so close to her that her
solidly constructed world seems to tremble. Don Ruggero di Credo, of course, is not affected by the opinions of others; but then, he is mad.

Alessandro Sarte, whose immaculate appearance implies a frequently consulted objective mirror at home,
is, perhaps, of all the characters, the most conscious
of his masks (Pl 217; E 73): physician (shared with
his colleagues); Roman profile (shared with the race
for two thousand years); sybarite and therefore most
eager to consult the mirror of another's gaze. He ur-
ges Marcella to continue her oral "biography" of him
Pl 218; E 74) and gives both to her images and to her
interpretation of them,the devoted attention that Narcissus gives his mirror. Differences of opinion between them require him to convince his mirror or to
readjust his mask.

Alessandro has an advantage over such characters
as Giulio and Miss Jones, in that his self-confidence
allows him to question, whereas weaker personalities
can only imagine what others think. Giulio finds Miss
Jones "an interesting young Englishwoman whom he had
hired out of sheer charity to help him during rush
hours...forgetting that he had looked a lot at Miss
Jones' slim, long legs" (Pl 180; E 21). Miss Jones
finds the gaze of all Italian men both an insult and a
danger (Pl 282; E 164). She trembles when she remembers the terrible scene made by the wife of this
"somewhat common though perfectly respectable merchant" (Pl 186; E 29). Giulio feels that she will
leave with the "image of a too-kind man who had been
unable to silence the ill-tempered Giuseppa" (Pl 189;
E 33) This interplay of opinions is a device that pro-
duces some of the most pathetic--and most humorous--
passages in **Denier**. The irony in the contrasts resulting from men's capacity for self-deception plays an

important role in the construction of the composite
picture the reader receives of each character.

At times some characters make a true effort to
communicate their inner reality. Because Massimo
claims to have recognized Clement Roux from a self-
portrait he recently saw, the artist believes that
Massimo can understand him. What he does not stop to
question, however, is whether the portrait is a mirror
or a mask. Each is feeling alone and depressed and
needs the other's sympathy and understanding, but when
he tries to communicate his innermost feelings, the
other is not listening (Pl 264 ff; E 138 ff). 4 Each
is alone looking into the mirror of his own soul.

Duality of character,Narcissus as contemplator and
reflection, is found throughout **Denier**. Mortally ill,
Lina Chiari recognizes the strange image she sees in a
store window as her own only because she recognizes
her clothing (Pl 175;E 14); Giuseppa Lovisi imagines a
seductive Giulio, more interesting than the near sexa-
genarian who is just barely able to dream of Miss
Jones as he wishes (Pl 180, 189; E 21, 33). Oreste
Marinunzi needs alcohol to see himself as he would
like and to forget the "other" Oreste whom no one
respects (Pl 283; E 165).

The characters in **Denier** serve as mirrors for each
other, and their views complete the picture that we
receive of them. We are introduced to Rosalia di Credo
first as she appears to Giulio (Pl 181 ff; E 22 ff)
and then as her neighbors see her "All this would have
been false" (Pl 189-90; E 35). As long as she can believe them false, she can go on living and keep her
real, i.e., dream life intact. In her room, however,
after learning that her ancestral home, Gemara, is to
be destroyed, she looks into a broken mirror, succinct
symbol of the disintegrated personality.There she sees
a stranger, someone who would say "yes" to her dreary
life, the Rosalia the others know. When this image has
been absorbed into the approaching night, Rosalia notices that she wants to die.

In the instances where someone is seen only as a
reflection in another's mirror, the reader can only

---

4. See also Pl 228ff (E 87ff) where Marcella and
    Massimo react in similar fashion.

guess at the accuracy of his image. During a scene (Pl 208-09; E 61-62), likened to a seance, each participant remembers Carlo Stevo, but he appears different in every case. Everyone evokes a "ghost" to inhabit a mirror reflecting a world where he too lives and fills a positive role. Vanna sees a great man who is sick (and the wife who both cares for and protects him in a world that she controls to accomodate him). Marcella sees a romantic hero indulging in cloak and dagger escapades (with herself as his faithful accomplice). Massimo sees a fugitive needing a false visa and affection (both of which Massimo can provide, thus giving himself a dominant role).

Mirrors are at their most powerful when they not only reflect, but act; when they themselves change what is reflected in them in order to achieve an unreality, a dream, which expresses the hidden nature of its subjects.

Yourcenar has herself stated her conviction that dreams are analogus to mirrors. In **Les Songes et les sorts** she describes the functions of the mirror as the correcting, the deforming or the reversing of images. These functions correspond to three types of dreams: (1) those that restore an idealized luster to life; (2) nightmares that give life a grotesque and frightening appearance; and (3) dreams whose inverted symbols conceal secret or dangerous truths. She adds: "Every dreamer is a Narcissus who is moved and fulfilled in front of an eternal mirror, and the minds of men who do not dream...[are] like rooms where there is no magic bay created by a mirror." [5] We recall too Hadrian's interest in dreams and his speculations on their meaning (Pl 512; E 291-92).

Dreams or daydreams readily compose life-like images which nevertheless exclude the realities of life. Rosalia imagines her sister, Angiola, returning to the apartment,disappointed in love and ready to allow herself to be cherished once more by her. She imagines their getting jobs as maids at Gemara, now a boarding house run by an Englishwoman. The real Angiola, whose ambitions include a glamorous career in Hollywood, is nowhere present in this dream. Only Rosalia's vision

---

5. Paris: Grasset, 1938, p. 21.

of her survives. Don Ruggero di Credo, their father, who lives in a world of unreality—or poetry—sees Angiola very differently. Although he has lived for some time in an asylum in Rome, his "real" life is in Sicily. For him, Angiola is still at Gemara "intact as the statues that, thanks to him, had emerged out of the earth's womb; statues to which he could compare her young naked beauty while she bathed in the woods in the Roman cistern" (Pl 203; E 53). The sinificance of the first part of the quotation will not escape the reader. The second involves the reverie that Gaston Bachelard discusses as "the woman at her bath" which, he reminds us, is an essentially unreal image. Although common in dreams and in art, it cannot exist objectively because the act of bathing disturbs the pure reflection. The dreamer, alone in the woods before the natural mirror of the lake or spring, projects his desire onto this mirror that gives both the ideal beauty and the innocence of water to the image. Absorbing the reflections, the water becomes in its substance the embodiment of the woman reflected in it.[6] The image of water's role clarifies our impression of Lina, first seen at the edge of a fountain (Pl 169; E 5); prepares the reader for the water in Angiola's film (Pl 241-46; E 106-13); and is most directly stated by Clement Roux. When he has filled his cupped hands with water from the fountain, he watches it trickle through his fingers and says, as though thinking aloud "Women's bodies..."(Pl 273; E. 151. Yourcenar's elipsis.).[7]

The most elaborate of the images that we shall consider here as idealizing mirrors is the film in which Angiola (the woman) watches herself as Angiola Fidès (the actress). The chapter opens (Pl 238; E 102) with Angiola's visiting the scenes of her childhood, trying to recapture the girl she once was. Nowhere in the novel is the theme of duality more apparent. The reader is prepared for considering the film as reflection in water by references references to "echo" and then to "forest" and "lake." The mirror is first suggested by the words "a mist that seemed to come from

---

6. Bachelard, p. 49.

7. The word "Women's," explicitly mentioned in the French version, is missing from the English translation.

her own breath" (Pl 240; E 105) recalling the words describing Lina's mirror (Pl 176; E 15). It is then named, as Angiola puts up a hand to adjust the coiffure worn by Angiola Fidès. We are reminded that the film is an idealized inner vision by the phrase "The magic room, crude reproduction of human memory" (Pl 240; E 105). Angiola Fidès, first the dream of an adolescent Angiola, now imitates the actions of "Narcissus at the edge of luminous waves"8 who, in turn, is seeking her reflection in the gestures of Angiola Fidès (Pl 241; E 106).

The image of the mask is introduced first as make-up (Pl 240; E 105) then appears explicitly when Angiola Fides' mouth opens like "a classical mask **pouring out floods of tragedy**" (Pl 241; E 106. Emphasis ours.)

There follows a scenario in which the film reflects Angiola's life, first her early experiences and then, in detail, the fictional present. A banal seduction scene in the theater loge progresses concurrently with, but in ironic contrast to, the (literally) grandiose romantic drama on the theater screen that serves the same function as a "mirror on a bedroom ceiling" "(Pl 246; E 112). Water images naturally dominate the entire passage, from "the sound of the waves" (Pl 241; E 106) to "the high waters of the dream invaded the room" (Pl 245; E 111), until finally "the great pleasure wave was spent, rose again, bringing the two drowned lovers to the surface"(Pl 246; E 112).

The distorting powers of the mirror can be either negative or positive--the reflection either nightmarish or grandiose. The eyes as infinitely large mirrors in which the subject appears as infinitely small are found in the 1934 edition: "She looked questioningly into those pupils--monstrous because they were so close--but saw nothing except the tiny reflection of a half-naked woman"(p. 24). This image was the last of a series expressing Lina's helplessness and fear in the doctor's office. The later editions retain the mirror image, but show Lina searching the doctor's eyes for clues to her inner, rather than outer state: "his gaze revealed nothing" (Pl 173; E 11). Memory and

---

8. In French the text reads "great female Narcissus."

frustrated hope combine in Giulio's picture of his wife, whose idiosyncrasies, he hoped, would moderarte with time. "On the contrary, as Giuseppa aged, her shortcomings grew as monstrous as her arms and waist" (Pl 179; E 20). In Angiola's film, "the enlarged reflection was of a gigantic kiss, blown open like a flower, suggesting, on the narrow space of lips and eyelids, the embrace of the whole body" (Pl 246; E 112), but the newsreel was "this repetition of [Alessandro's] nightmare" (Pl 244; E 110).

Distortion to produce great size is found particularly in images of the dictator, whose role Marguerite Yourcenar describes as essentially "a huge political shadow that is cast" (Pl 164; E 173). In the 1934 edition, Massimo tells Marcella: "You are going to make that man (that human puppet) larger than life with your hatred as others...have done with their fervor" (p. 138). Alessandro, who sees the dictator in person, later describes his memory of the incident as a nightmare spent waiting to see whether or not Marcella would actually make her assassination attempt. When Alessandro sees him in a newsreel at the Cinema Mondo, as a gigantic figure on the screen, the real man's relationship to his image is compared to the "shreds of reality still rising at night on the edge of sleep" (Pl 244-45; E 110).

In the closing passages of the book the reflection moves beyond the looking-glass, beyond natural water, to the organic image of wine. As Oreste looks into his glass, unhappy images become small and distant, while grandiose visions of himself arise. To console himself for his problems in life, he orders rum with his wine. Then, in the manner of drunkenness and dreams, he passes with dizzying speed through a number of metamorphoses: he becomes first rich, then compassionate, powerful, wise, and finally unconscious.

Symbolic mirrors or dreams are likewise frequent. Don Ruggero is, himself,"a cracked mirror" of his race (Pl 191; E 37) and in his palm can be read,not his future, for he has none, but the past of all those who have gone before him. The dictator has the symbolic value of "a false god," and his death would be "Caesar's apotheosis" (Pl 230; E 91). The fountain into which Clement Roux throws the coin is yet another symbolic mirror. Seated by its edge, he would normally see in it a sick, old man, but this fountain unites the forces of nature and the art of man (Pl 272; E

149-50). The mythological figures that gave both the water and the rock an artificial appearance have been eroded through the years, so that the statues once more seem to be only the stone from which they were carved, and the water seems natural in its setting. It is an island that adds the virtues of its natural and elemental forces to the surrounding city. Its sound, its purity, and its legend (of bringing travelers back to Rome) make it a fountain of youth to a tired and distressed man who needs its reassurance and its promise.

In the mirror world of unreality, time does not, of course, exist in the same framework as it does outside. The reason that Lina, for example, fails to recognize her image in Giulio's shop window is that the face she knows belongs to the past whereas the one she sees belongs to the future, when sickness will have brought her to hospitals that "serve as cold borders of death" (Pl 175; E 14). The "ghost" vanishes under her lipstick mask, and Lina becomes once more very much alive (Pl 176; E 15); Mother Dida, who, when young, "had looked like a flower; now...looked like a tree trunk" (Pl 250;E 119) catches sight of herself in the mirror as she approaches the door of the washroom that the cafe owner allows her to use. As an integrated personality, she does not divide her past and present, but takes pleasure in the reflection of an old woman "who, Dida knew, would have made heads turn thirty years ago" (Pl 258; E 129-30).

Of all the symbolic mirrors in **Denier**,the most notable, and the most fully developed, is Gemara. It is the outward and visible sign of an inner realization of home--"cemented by blood;" the house was only "a symbol in stone" (Pl 193; E 40,47).[9] This six hundred year-old house reflects the changes produced by the elements and by the differing tastes of generations of the di Credos. It is a universe apart, with its climate, its own laws (Pl 193; E 40),existing outside the time continuum applicable to what others call reality (Pl 191-92; E 37-38). So perfect is the vision that it could only be a reflection in water. In the 1934 edition, Gemara was located on a river bank; although

---

9.
    In French this reads "an unnecessary proof in stone."

the reflection was not--did not need to be--mentioned. In the later edition the reverie is interiorized, and the only water present is the "dark waters" to which the recesses of Don Ruggero's mind are compared (Pl 192; E 39).

That Gemara is a behind-the-looking-glass world is amply demonstrated when one broken window destroys Don Ruggero's illusion and makes him, temporarily, amenable to leaving (Pl 196; E 45). At the asylum he can rediscover Gemara, he has only to trade in "his mind for his own universe" (Pl 203; E 54). When Rosalia wishes to return, she carefully closes the windows of her apartment in Rome and waits until darkness has removed the reflection of her realistic self (Pl 204-06; E 56-58). These two, as others who inhabit mirror worlds, are judged mad by those living on the other side of the glass.

Gemara possesses magic power in that it can form its occupants in its own image (Pl 191; E 37). It is at the center of a dreamer's world, i.e., in the interior of an island. The painful and difficult crossing of the waters when leaving (Pl 198; E 47) or returning to it (Pl 205-06; E 57) is evident in its symbolism and attests to the relationship of Gemara to the rest of the world and to life itself.

Rosalia had taken upon herself all the pain and misfortunes of her life and the lives of her family. What she could not stand was the loss of the security of a Gemara separated from herself only by space. The legal papers announcing its destruction were equivalent to her own death notice (Pl 203; E 54). While she understood that Gemara was within herself, distant in time, not space; and although she had destroyed and rebuilt it differently twenty times in her imagination; yet she is no longer strong enough alone to protect this image of the family, and rather than lose it, she chooses to die. In a dream sequence (Pl 203-06; E 54-58), all of the four material elements are evoked, and raised to a cosmic level, to celebrate the death of this woman, whose devotion allows her to surpass her sister, Angiola, in beauty.

The mirrors thus far considered have a central figure whom we see in his own world. Their accumulation allows us a composite, but still somewhat fragmented, view of larger groups. Universal mirrors are needed to facilitate comparisons and generalizations.

41

Art, history, and tradition serve this function for society as a whole. Each person sees in them his values, his dreams, and his memories. By comparing these reflections, we can draw conclusions about each individual and his relationship with others.

The Litany of the Virgin in the church of Santa Maria Minore is an early example of a general mirror, although, since it is recited,it is perhaps more properly the function of Echo, the companion of Narcissus, and another doubling image. It is the voice of water, always youthful and fresh, present in springs and fountains (cf Pl 169; E 5). Each character present seizes upon one of the phrases and pursues his own line of thought:"Queen of Martyrs" makes Marcella conscious of her coming assassination attempt; "Queen of Heaven" (Regina Coeli) is the name of a Roman prison. "Tower of ivory" makes Clement Roux think of the most beautiful girl's body he ever saw. "Singular vessel" reminds Giulio that he forgot to get some medecine on the way home. "Queen of Virgins" embarrasses Miss Jones again as she thinks of the scene Giulio's wife made and of the suspicions that cost her her temporary job in his shop. It is apparent from this scene that although they are presumably engaged in a act of common worship, each is intrinsically alone, and further that they see in everything reflections of their most immediate concerns. The irony of the situation is clearly the exalted view of humanity, as represented by the attributes of the Virgin and by the mystical love of the writer of the litany, compared with the primarily physical or mundane problems of these worshippers. Even "ORAPRONOBIS" at the end is disputed, in that Marcella sees the unquestioning acceptance that such formulae imply; and Miss Jones, overcome by the sentimentality of the atmosphere, regrets not being Catholic. This little group's reactions are further put in perspective by historical references both before and after the litany (Pl 184; E 26 and Pl 187; E 31) to the invocations and ceremonies that generations of suffering humanity have used to protect themselves from the world.

Statues and other works of art reflect huamnity's qualities and constitute a mirror embracing all time. Human characters are often compared to them.10 Given

_____

10. See, for example, Pl 175; E 14 (Lina); Pl 190; E 35 (Rosalia); Pl 191; E 37 (Don

that what is **seen** also **sees**, as Bachelard has pointed
outll we must imagine that the statues evoked in the
church (Pl 180-81; E 22), at Gemara (Pl 194;E 41-42),
in the museum in Palermo (Pl 203; E 53), and in Rome
(Pl 238; E 100 and Pl 279; E 159) contemplate the
crowds who come to view them. Since they represent
sublimations of human beauty and character traits,
such reciprocal contemplation constitutes both comparison and a major ironic contrast. The natural acceptance of this reciprocity is noted in the movie scene,
when spectators applaud "unable to believe in the
deafness of this eloquent face" (Pl 241; E 106).

   History fills this same dual role in the novel;
the ruins of the forums mask both the squalor of the
poorer sections of the city (Pl 239-40; E 103-04) and
the hollow glitter of the Cinema Mondo. Their relatively small size, sufficient to perpetuate the memory
of ancient Rome, makes the huge boulevards (constructed for busses, or,if the need arises, for tanks) seem
pretentious (Pl 263; E 137). Clement Roux, who makes
this judgment and finds the Rome of 1933 ugly by comparison with the Rome of his youth, is not merely, in
Horace's words, a **laudator temporis acti** 'praiser of
time past' he thinks the stray cats, killed when ren-
ovations were undertaken, as interesting as "a stack
of dead Caesars" (Pl 262; E 136). Yet Caesar does play
a role in **Denier,** for the dictator is not only called,
but also thinks of himself as Caesar (Pl 230; E 91 and
Pl 277; E 156). The irony of this comparison, already
evident in 1934, loomed significantly larger in 1959,
when the novel was rewritten, because the readers knew
the entire career and the death of this man who tried
to put on Caesar's mask, the better to wear his
laurels.

   Finally, **Denier** is, in itself, a mirror. One of
its major themes, and some of the criticism on it,
concerns life in a fascist state, as Madame Yourcenar
notes in her preface to the work (Pl 163-65; E 172-
74). Valuable as such a mirror was, or is, however,

   Ruggero); Pl 204; 56 (Marcella); Pl 228; E
   88 (Massimo); Pl 265; E 140 (Rome); and Pl
   273; E 151 (Angiola).

11. Bachelard, pp. 42 ff.

we do not believe this to be its principal virtue. Works too narrowly focussed on the political realities of an era pass with it. **Denier,** on the contrary, has much broader implications, as the author no doubt sensed when she decided to allow "Caesar" to remain vague, an oppressive shadow. The last chapter, a kind of epilogue, shows the characters at night without their masks or other kinds of mirrors. Moreover, it integrates them with the rest of Rome—other people, but also buildings, animals and art—and with the world, considered in its substance.

This novel will not age because it mirrors not merely the Eternal City, but the eternal city. In it we see human beings coming to grips with—or trying to ignore—problems that change in form, but which, beneath their current mask, remain the same.It is a magic mirror, reflecting beauty, pathos, humor, and wisdom. Within its frame we can see not only objective reality, but the inner workings of the spirit, the past trials, successes and failures of man, his ever-present striving for understanding, for action, for affirmation of his intrinsic worth. We also see his myths, his dreams, his abject fear, his stubborn hope, his reaching for a future that are all as eternal as his city.

Note on **Feux**

Feux (1936) is like **Denier du rêve** in a number of respects. It too relies heavily on myth and dream to lift it beyond the specific and the mundane; it too is written in a lyrical, impressionistic style. Unlike **Denier**, it has not been rewritten, except for the occasional retouching of an image; Yourcenar has maintained that the same stylistic traits that were confusing when used to describe a whole society are eminently suitable for a book that is partly a confession partly a search for eternal values through individual experience.

The book is one which defies convenient classification by literary genre. The aphorisms belong to the same category as journals, but at the same time are related to maxims, like those of La Rochefoucauld. The sketches have been called short stories; they have also been called prose poems. In its expression and its make-up, the book is as intensely personal as the love that inspired it.

Feux was written in the period of Marguerite Yourcenar's life, 1934-36, when she lived much of the time in Greece, whose ambiance forms the background of the book. In it the author tells the story--obliquely--of a love affair beginning in joy and confidence and progressing to anger, bitterness, despair, and finally the decision of the persona to rebuild her life.

Because of the complexity of its stylistic effects and the apparent lack of continuity between aphorisms and stories and among the stories themselves, critical reactions to this book have ordinarily remained of the most general kind. Seen in its details, however, this book may be demonstrated to be a very tightly woven complex with a discernible pattern.

The principal differences among the five editions of **Feux** from 1936 to 1982, lie in the introduction. The English version, entitled **Fires**, was published in 1981.

Feux: Structure and Meaning

Feux is a lyrical volume on love containing ten groups of **pensées** alternating with nine stories, first written in 1935, when the author was 32.[1] In it, as she explains in the prefatory note to the original edition, "The author has mingled **pensées**, which were the theorums of passion for her, with stories that illustrate, explain and often mask them."

While their beauty is a sufficient raison d'etre for these, as for any poems, the volume, taken as a whole, has still another. We wish to show how the elements in **Feux** are ordered and how the resulting structure gives added meaning to the whole and to each of the parts. **Feux** is both part and product of a journey of self-discovery, and it is in relation to this quest that we shall consider its most important images and themes.

Since the **pensées**, taken primarily from the author's diary, and nearly all of the stories, were first published separately, it is clear that they each have meaning when considered independently of the others.[2] Yet it is important to note first that the **pensées** were rearranged when they were combined with

1. Paris: Grasset, 1936; rpt. in **Oeuvres romanesques** (Paris: Gallimard, 1982). All references, unless otherwise noted, are to this Pléiade edition. **Fires**, trans. Dori Katz in collaboration with the author (New York: Farrar, Straus, and Giroux, 1981).

2. "Feux," **Revue de France**, 4 (1935), 491-98 (This is a first version of the **pensées.**); "Deux Amours d'Achille," **Mercure de France**, 263 (1935), 118-27 (This reference includes the stories now called "Achille" and "Patrocle."); "Antigone-Phèdre," **Revue Politique et Littéraire: Revue Bleue** (1936), pp. 442-45; "Aveux de Clytemnestre," **Revue de France**, 3 (1936), 54-62; "Complainte de Marie-Madeleine," **Cahiers du Sud** (1936), pp. 129-37; "Suicide de Sappho," **Cahiers du Sud** (1936), pp. 801-11.

the tales and secondly that, despite a considerable number of stylistic revisions for later editions, no change has occurred in the order either of the **pensées** or of the tales, from the 1936 edition to the present.3

The protagonists of all the tales have known an all-consuming love--one that could serve to fill a life. Their voices exult, postulate, demand, respond, supplicate, deny, interact with each other and with the voice heard in the **pensées**. This persona does not narrate, but suggests a personal love story, from its happy beginning: "The admirable Paul was wrong...There is...for each love...a singularly strong stimulant-- THE ENTIRE REST OF THE WORLD--which is opposed to it and is not worthy of it (Pl 1051; E 3. Author's emphasis); to painful despair: "Burned with more fires... Worn-out beast...a hot whip lashes my back" (Pl 1089; E 61); to acceptance and transcendency in the end: "One can only raise happiness on a foundation of despair. I think I will be able to start building" (Pl 1135; E 130).

In addition the reader hears in some of the tales, e.g. "Clytemnestra," and between many of the **pensées**, another voice, that of the interlocutor--for here there is a dialogue, a drama, of which we read only the response and must imagine the rest. Perhaps they are but one voice, speaking in different accents, with different inflections, as were the many voices Theseus heard in the labyrinth.4

Feux reminds us of a mosaic, or better, a kaleidoscope in which the images, colors, and motifs form designs around given axes--in this case,the great themes of love--but which constantly shift and form new designs. The elements in the compositions thus formed may be identical or similar words whose repetition forms a bond among two or more stories, or with the **pensées**. For example, the words "irremplaçable" 'irreplaceable' and "irréparable" 'irreparable,' similar in

3. Phaedra, Achilles, Patroclus, Antigone, Lena, Mary Magdalene, Phaedo, Clytemnestra, Sappho.

4. "Qui n'a pas son Minotaure?" in **Théâtre II** (Paris: Gallimard, 1971).

sound and used to convey the same emotion, tie together "Mary Magdalene," "Phaedo," and "Clytemnestra." "Servir" 'serve' appears in the **pensées** (Pl 1073; E 33) and is related to the "servante" 'servant' throughout both "Lena" and "Clytemnestra." Colors, the four elements, certain archetypal images, image clusters—all are leit-motifs that serve as implicit comparisons which illuminate and enrich each occurrence with the values of the others.

Too much space would be required to examine in detail all of the intricate image patterns which are repeated—with subtle variations throughout Feux. Two examples, one relatively simple, and one a cluster, are offered here merely to suggest their nature and complexity. The bronze armor of Patroclus (Pl 1062; E 18) becomes in the next story (Pl 1072; E 32) Penthesilea's golden armor that is taken from her after death—an image that is repeated in "Antigone" where Polynices is recognizable because his body, too has been stripped (Pl 1077; E 40). Beginning with the golden armor image, we note that, when the visor is removed a "Mask with blind eyes" is revealed (Pl 1072; E 32). From there we might go to other theater images, or to the theme of blindness in "Antigone," "Phaedo," and the **pensées** (Pl 1065-66; E 23-24; Pl 1079; E 44).

Images clustering about the acrobat would constitute a study in themselves; we will only suggest their ramifications. Sappho is an acrobat, as she used to be a poet, because of her affinities with the elements of air and earth. Yet, she "dives" from her trapeze and water imagery predominates in the remainder of the story. The acrobat, as a symbol of inversion, invokes the exchange of masculine and feminine characteristics essential to "Achilles," "Patroclus," "Clytemnestra," and "Sappho." The very nature of her profession necessitates our considering in this connection images of lightness and flight and their contraries; weight, vertigo, the fall,[5] and death, of which there are innumerable examples. The milieu of this drama of

---

5. For examples of these images see the following: weight Pl 1051;E 3, Pl 1078; E 43, Pl 1091; E 64; vertigo Pl 1063; E 20; fall Pl 1058; E 11, Pl 1090; E 62, Pl 1098-99; E 76-77, Pl 1120; E 110.

flight and fall is space or the void,6 and water (to
denote space, depth, time and death). The acrobat is
further identified throught height with the bird and,
in the **pensées**, with a modern equivalent, the
airplane.7 Other winged creatures like angels and
statues of Victory add their nuances.8 The climbing up the ladder to the acrobat's trapeze, described
as transcending the human condition (Pl 1132-33; E
127-29), is related to Jacob's ladder (Pl 1090; E
62). This last image and others tie the cluster to images of God and of sacrifice (always associated by
symbolic logic with inversion) which will be discussed
later.

A cursory discussion of one cluster serves to illustrate our point on their complexity. Similar clusters form around such major images and themes as wine,
stars, fire, life, love, and many others.

The relationships established by these leit-motifs
are themselves part of a larger whole. The philosophical and psychological weight and the oneiric
value of the images, as well as the character, setting
and plot of the tales, contribute to furthering the
basic theme of **Feux**, namely a journey, a quest, a
descent into the self (or into Hell) and the return.
This is the frame-work that all the elements over-
lie. To achieve this impression, the author has
carefully structured the book, distributing and bal-
ancing its components so that the second half
echoes and mirrors the first half, but has a more

---

6. cf. e.g. Pl 1054; E 8, Pl 1063; E 20-21, Pl 1093;
   E 66-67, Pl 1112; E 96, Pl 1117; E 104, Pl 1126; E
   116, Pl 1132-33; E 127-28.

7. For examples see: the bird Pl 1057; E 10, Pl 1063;
   E 21, Pl 1104; E 83; the airplane Pl 1057; E 10,
   Pl 1102; E 79, Pl 1113; E 98.

8. For examples see: angels Pl 1097; E 74, Pl 1102; E
   79; statues of Victory Pl 1063-64; E 21-22, Pl
   1081; E 48, Pl 1083; E 50.The symbolic values of
   the images in this cluster are too well- known to
   require explanation. The page references have
   been given to show that the images occur
   throughout **Feux** and to allow the interested reader
   to examine this relationship more closely.

positive emphasis. The over-all effect may be represented as an inverted bell-shaped curve.

"Phaedra" and "Sappho," the first and the last of the tales, present differing perspectives on suicide. Phaedra, based on the heroine of Racinc's play rather than the Greek model, does not regret having loved, for, with the same shock we experience on first reading Camus' **The Myth of Sisyphus**, we find that her final reaction is "Thank-you." Yet she commits suicide, because she sees an image of herself that she despises and finds herself in a situation with which she cannot cope. Sappho, on the other hand, comes to the realization that no matter whom she loves, the affair will always be a repetition of the joy, but also the hurt and despair, she has experienced with Attys. She attempts suicide by climbing to the kind of height attainable only in dreams, intending to fall to her death. She does not succeed. Her art, i.e. her skill as an acrobat, which she thought she had deserted, saves her. Repeated attempts to miss the trapeze fail, and when she finally jumps, it is to land safely in the net. The only way she has "gone beyond" herself is by attaining the impossible height. The final **pensée** comments on this destiny: It is not a question of suicide. It is only a question of beating a record" (Pl 1135; E 130).

In the second and eighth stories, "Achilles" and "Clytemnestra," respectively, the protagonists each commit murder, another violent act, but not surprising, since violence is never far from the surface in **l'amour fou** 'mad love.' Achilles, whom his mother had hidden in Lycomedes' castle, that he might escape his fate at Troy, is disguised in women's clothing, and both looks like and thinks of himself as a woman. He is confronted with two women, one masculine in nature, the other feminine. With the arrival of the kings who are searching for him,he is suddenly faced with Patroclus and recognizes in the kings' voices, his own conscience. Achilles strangles Deidamia, the more feminine of the two women, thus symbolically killing one half of his own nature, the dark and emotional side-- his anima. By so doing, he is able to accept his masculine role. In "Clytemnestra," the queen has spent

the ten years of the Trojan War fulfilling the functions that her husband normally carried out. A strong
and resourceful woman, she has by now so identified
herself with Agamemnon that she may be viewed as killing another embodiment of the male half of her person
ality--the animus. The differences between the two
murders are clearly demonstrated by the way in which
they were performed. Achilles strangles Deidamia
"like a girl...he used his hands" (Pl 1062; E 18) in a
blind passion, and then escapes from the tower only
with help from Misandra, the more masculine girl, to
sail for Troy. By contrast, the woman, Clytemnestra,
commits a well-planned, well-executed murder with a
masculine weapon, an axe. She does it to avenge herself for the wrongs done her, and in order to affirm
her worth: to be, not a thing, but a full person in
her own right.

"Patroclus" is a counterpart of "Achilles," for in
it Achilles kills a second woman, a second love. The
first murder was, as we have seen, feminine with respect to manner, place, weapon, and victim. The second is a masculine murder: it is done with a sword, on
the field of battle, and he kills the Amazon queen, a
masculine woman, who, he discovered too late, was
"worthy of being a friend...the only creature in the
world who looked like Patroclus (Pl 1072; E 32). His
weapon, the blade, links this second story with "Clytemnestra" as well.

"Patroclus" and "Phaedo," the third and seventh
stories, deal, more than any of the others, with the
annihilation of time and space. In "Patroclus" Achilles and Penthesilea begin their epic duel against the
background of the Trojan War, but, in the manner of
dreams, setting and costume shift and change, reflecting the ages through which such struggles have gone
on, uninterrupted. In alternating adagio and allegro
movements, the two fighters perform a kind of ballet,
advancing and retreating, until finally the tragic
climax is reached with Penthesilea's death. Phaedo,
Socrates' disciple dances three times in the course of
the story: at first, in his youth, out of sheer joy
(Pl 1104; E 83); a second time after his enslavement,
"Each time my heel hit the dirty floor, I drove my
past...further into the ground...my desperate dancing
trampled Phaedo under my feet." (Pl 1107; E 88); a
third time at the end of the story when, by his dance,
he rises above the circumstances of his life,his ambitions,his attachment to Socrates, and moral judgments,

to attain a level of cosmic awareness where his dance alone can fill the universe (Pl 1112; E 96-97). The dances in these two stories--surely reminiscent of Shiva's dancing over the world, abolishing forms and creating them anew--illustrate, as does "Sappho," the creative force of art and the conquering of space and time.

Antigone (in the fourth story) and Mary Magdalene (in the sixth) portray two facets of the search for the absolute. As in the Greek myth, Antigone is less a young woman than a moral force. She protects her blind father, Oedipus; buries her brother, Polynices; but rejects her fiance, Haemon, because of the possibility of having to bring children into a world of compromise. Although she loves all three, it is not her love, but an ideal, that serves as the motivating force behind her actions. She sets an example of purity, justice, and charity, but hers is the "terrible virginity of not being of this world" (Pl 1077; E 40). Mary Magdalene, on the other hand, who sets out to seduce God in order to regain the devotion of her husband, John the Apostle, comes to see in Christ someone who shares with her "the terrible lot of belonging to all" (Pl 1095; E 71).

Through helping him in his "scandalous Messiah profession" (Pl 1094; E 69), even to accepting the role of dishwasher at the Last Supper, Mary Magdalene realizes that her suffering, humiliation, and loss in this world are what will allow her to attain salvation. To give yourself no more is to give yourself still," says the persona of the **pensées** "for you are giving your sacrifice" (Pl 1073; E 3).

With Lena--the concubine of Aristogiton, who plotted with Harmodius to overthrow the dictator, Hipparchus--we reach the lowest point in **Feux.** Her unquestioning adoration of her master allows her to share him with Harmodius, to accept the lowliest tasks, but without the same consolations that Mary Magdalene will have and, the final humiliation, to do all these things without needing to share in his secrets. After the plot fails, and Hipparchus wants information about it, Lena, who is facing torture, cuts out her tongue so that she will not have to make "the humiliating confession that she was just a servant and not an accomplice" (Pl 1088; E 60). "There is between us something better than love: a complicity," the persona exulted in the first group of pensées (Pl 1051; E 3); following Lena, she says, "I will not fall, I have reached the center..." (Pl 1090; E 62).

Two of the pensees, depicting nights of the soul, deserve attention. Their placement in **Feux** helps to support our hypothesis of balanced structure. While they were at first in reverse order, coming close together and near the end of the sequence, they were put in the book so as to contribute to its symetry, following the first two and preceding the last two stories. The first of them (Pl 1066; E 24-25) divides "Phaedra" and "Achilles," where the protagonists try to escape their destinies, from "Patroclus" and "Antigone," where the principals, if they are not able to find positive solutions, are at least capable of facing their problems and themselves. In this passage, the persona describes an extraordinary realization of the nature of sleep. Water images with all their connotations of birth, journey, and death, make explicit the difference between the sleep of a person consoled by love and one deprived of it. "The other day" (any unspecified time when she was loved), "drunk with happiness," (intoxicated by, and avid for, happiness) she threw herself on her bed with the confidence of a back diver and floated on her back over an abyss she did not see, secure in her air-filled lungs. "I emerged from this Greek sea like a new-born island." All of water's life-giving virtues radiate from the first half of this passage. Then, suddenly, "Tonight," (the terrible present of her despair), "glutted with unhappiness," (the negative of intoxication) 9 she collapses on her bed like a drowning victim who is giving up; sleep becomes asphyxiation. Immediately the water changes complexion. It is bitter and salty, like tears. She compares herself to a mummy, floating in its solution, afraid of awakening to what could only be survival, i.e. living beyond her real death. Dreams and memories become debris, floating in the current, on which she hurts herself as they pass. She is cold.

---

9. The fact that the English word "glut" is often used for food must not be allowed to obscure the contrast between the French words "ivre" (intoxicated) and "saoule" (drunk).

The second of these traumatic nights (Pl 1114; E
99-100) shifts, in the same way as do the stories in
the second half, from initial despair to a more positive ending. It also divides the stories about Mary
Magdalene and Phaedo, who are led to see value in
their experience, from those of Clytemnestra and Sappho, the strongest and most forceful characters in
Feux, who suffer and question, but who then work out
their own solution and accept their destiny. In this
pensée she tells of a night spent walking. At 2 AM she
is so tired that she no longer remembers that she is
trying to forget. In parable form she tells of rescue
and new beginnings and imagines an "old man" coming to
her across a river (which surely belongs to the Underworld), carrying a precious gift. She does not know
exactly what it will be, but it will be enough to
"change everything:" "a bird, a seed, a knife, a key"
--all are symbols of inspiration, regeneration, or release. These two passages are perhaps the most lyrical
in **Feux** and are excellent self-contained illustration
of Marguerite Yourcenar's style and how it reflects
her thought.

We have described **Feux** as a journey of self-discovery; it may also be compared expressly to a certain
type of self-discovery, namely, initiation rites in
which the candidate learns the mysteries taught by a
god.[10] This hypothesis is based primarily upon the
close relationship between the beloved and god in **Feux**
e.g. "You are God." (Pl 1090; E 62), but it is supported by a passage in one of her recent books, **Souvenirs pieux** (1974), in which a nineteenth-century
bedroom is called the "Cave of the Mysteries," showing
that Marguerite Yourcenar still thinks of love in
these terms. In **Les Charités d'Alcippe (The Alms of
Alcippe)**[11] one can find even more specific references
to ancient rites. "Idoles" (p. 16; E 17) mentions

---

10. For further discussion of these rites, see M.
    Esther Harding, **Women's Mysteries Ancient and
    Modern** (New York: Harper and Row, 1976), to which
    we acknowledge our debt.

11. Liège: La Flûte enchantée, 1956. **The Alms of
    Alcippe**, trans. Edith R. Farrell (New York: Targ
    Editions, 1982).

roses, which may be supposed to be the roses of Isis; and,in the next poem,"Vers orphiques," "Orphic Verses" there appears the formula once given to initiates of Osiris to guarantee their safe passage through the realm of the dead: "I am the son of the black earth." (p.16; E 18). In the Preface to **Feux** itself, Madame Yourcenar states her conviction that "absolute love" is imbued with a sort of mystical virtue and that it is meaningless unless associated in some way with the idea of transcendency(Pl 1043;E 10).

Feux seems to us to be related to the mysteries of the Moon Goddess in which women candidates sacrificed themselves in the **hieros gamos**, or sacred union with the god. This rite was performed in three stages,following broad outlines which are common to most initiations and for which parallels may be seen in **Feux**. After an initial withdrawal, the candidate undergoes transformation and purification by suffering, and, finally, re-birth and re-integration into society with a new perspective. It must not be thought that **Feux** systematically retraces the various stages of these ancient rites,and that exact relationships exist between it and the cults' ceremonies. Nevertheless, they have enough elements in common to justify the comparison as illustrative of the significance that Marguerite Yourcenar places on love.

Withdrawal is plainly symbolized first in Phaedra's abandoning both Crete, which repelled her, and Theseus' well-ordered world where passions like hers did not exist. Secondly, it appears in Achilles' two refuges: Lycomedes' tower and his own tent that is equivalent to a tomb. The **pensées** also tell us of isolation. Anyone who can say, "On a plane, next to you, I am no longer afraid. One dies only alone" (Pl 1057; E 10) is untouched by the world, is in a state of euphoria that denies reality. Not only joy,but sickness, to which Madame Yourcenar has compared love, can cut its victims off and reduce them to concentrating on the state of their health. The passage on the sanitarium (Pl 1065; E 23) is reminiscent of **The Magic Mountain.**

The relationship with god is a pervading theme in **Feux**. Both in the **pensées** and in the tales, the beloved is frequently called a god, although the characteristics that elicit this comparison and the value judgments placed on it vary considerably. In one place God is everything that we cannot overcome (Pl 1090; E

62); in another the persona says ironically: "You have just enough beauty, blindness and exactingness to incarnate an all-powerful" (Pl 1111; E 98). God is sometimes the Christian God (cf. Pl 1089; E 61, Pl 1102; E 79-80) and "Mary Magdalene"), sometimes one or several of the Greek gods, as Lena, for example,sees Harmodius successively as Apollo (Pl 1084; E 52), Hermes (Pl 1085; E 54), Nemesis (Pl 1086; E 56), and Bacchus (Pl 1084; E 57). Although a mortal is bound to be not only defeated, but broken and radically changed in the struggle, measuring himself against god is nonetheless the only way that he can rise. Mary Magdalene states it most directly: "I did right in letting the great divine wave spin me; I don't regret being refashioned by the Lord's hands" (Pl 1099; E 77), echoing the persona of the **pensées** who has already said: "The steps of the golden staircase are only for those who first accept this eternal undoing" (Pl 1090; E 62).

The **hieros gamos** was a sacred marriage through which the woman initiate experienced her own instincts and desires to the fullest. In this stage she was pushed to her limit and obliged to accept her nature without being able to defend or justify her reactions as a response to her partner's tenderness, since he was a priest, or even a stranger staying in the temple, who represented the god. A stranger filling this role was obliged to leave before daybreak to insure that no emotional bond was formed. The candidate had to know her unconscious as the source of her emotions and pass through this mass of instincts to arrive at a union with the masculine principle that would allow her to order, reflect upon, and ultimately control them.

The experience of the power of instinct and desire is illustrated in the first three stories. Phaedra yields, in spite of herself, to her incestuous passion. Achilles, in his disguise and in his combat with Penthesilea, illustrates the male candidate who must explore the feminine side of his nature: "All his life, Achilles had taken women to represent the instinctive part of misfortune, the one he did not choose, but had to endure" (Pl 1071; E 30).

In the **pensées** the exploration of pleasure devoid of tenderness is criticized when the partner is merely another mortal since the result seems to be either debauchery (Pl 1089; E 61) or egocentricity (Pl 1073; E 33). However, the desire aroused by love is depicted as continuing when reciprocated love is no longer a justification. The extent of the desolation and suffering caused by it is expressed in one of the most poignant sentences of **Feux**: "I rediscovered the true meaning of the poetic metaphors" (Pl 1089; E 61).

That the persona was pushed to the limits of her endurance is ackowledged in "You are God; you could break me" (Pl 1090; E 62) and by her reference to torture and degradation on the preceding page. It will be noted that this series of **pensées** follows "Lena" and is therefore at the lowest point of the descent described in **Feux**.

Lena, herself, is capable of adoration and devotion without demanding a corresponding passion on her lover's part. The ironic persona says: "I bear your faults. One is resigned to God's faults. I bear your lacks. One is resigned to God's lacks! (Pl 1066-67; E 25).12

The second stage in the initiation rites is a sacrifice, perceived variously by different cults. It is the giving up of the special relationship with the beloved: the possessive feeling toward a lover or the maternal one toward a son. In some cases it involved an actual or symbolic killing of the beloved.

The lesson that the candidate had to learn at this stage is that the love relationship, which is at first perceived as intensely personal, is in fact impersonal. The sacred union is only one manifestation of the life force. An individual person is only one embodiment of this force, and, like her act, is significant only in relation to the whole.

The idea of sacrifice, so clear with regard to a god, is a difficult one to accept in normal human relationships, and, while it is introduced relatively

---

12. "Bear"is here "to put up with" not "to be responsible for." The ironic contrast between the singular and the plural of the same word "defaut" is lost in English. An alternate translation might read: "I can put up with your faults. A person gets resigned to God's faults. I can put up with your default. A person gets resigned to God's default."

58

early in the **pensées** and in the stories, it does not progress without moments of denial, nor does it become a dominant theme until near the end of the book.

It is this theme that makes the transition from the more ego-centered characters of Phaedra and Achilles to the other-directed ones, of whom Antigone and Lena are the first. While the latter sacrifice themselves and their love (Antigone to justice and Lena to the men alone without needing to understand them), the idea of sacrificing the sacrifice does not come until Mary Magdalene.

While at the beginning of the story Mary Magdalene can imagine her life in no terms other than daily, routine "happiness" with an individual lover, she changes so radically that, at the end, she is glad that her love for Christ has allowed her to escape those "routines": marriages, children, and old age surrounded by descendants spent in peaceful somnolence, no longer having to strive. These are the very things that are, for so many, the high points of their lives and the consolation for their ills. She gave up her possessive love, and has received only the dark side of the joys in life; yet it is through them that she can attain salvation. The persona says succinctly: "How dull it would have been to be happy!" (Pl 1123; E 113).

The third, and most important, stage in the rites is thought to have required that the candidate ask the meaning of the symbols she had seen. The will to understand is what enables the initiate to benefit from her experiences. If she can realize that her unconscious is the past and the source of her emotions, than she can control the present and have insight into the future, thus releasing herself from dependency on time. The immortality conferred by these rites is not a permanent state of bliss, peace, or nothingness, but, in accordance with the nature of the Moon, eternal change: a waxing and waning, creation and destruction, in an endless cycle. The result of her ardor may be a human child--one type of immortality--or, if the creative energy is absorbed into the self, then the product may be instead, a work of art. In either case, it is the **act** of creation that is more important than what is created because it is in creating that we discover ourselves.

59

The later stories: "Phaedo," "Clytemnestra," and
"Sappho," continue to develop the theme of sacrifice,
but they also illustrate the release from time peculiar to the third stage. Phaedo sacrifices first
childlike joy, then his illusions about Alcibiades,
then his love for Socrates in exchange for the abstract wisdom which in turn becomes unimportant, when,
in his final dance, he goes beyond time and space. Although the persona does not find it easy to free herself from this concept: "Ah, to die in order to stop
Time" (Pl 1102; E 80), the author moves from this pensée directly to "Phaedo" which illustrates one way in
which it may be done. Clytemnestra clearly exemplifies
the sacrifice of the god/lover. She calls the young
Agamemnon a god and describes her relationship with
him as adoration and service. Acting out the myth of
the goddess, she kills a god (cf. her comparison of
him to a bull, and of his death to a ritual sacrifice,
Pl 1120; E 110) who will be born again and continue to
repeat this cycle forever (Pl 1121; E 111-12).

"Sappho" tells of the sacrifice of a lover/son but
it also serves to reiterate all of the major themes of
the initiation lessons. Sappho's lover is a woman, but
she is named Attys, the same as Cybele's consort. Sappho's mothering role is emphasized since Attys is almost totally dependent on her and is described as
though she were a child. When Attys "dies," by run-
ning away, Sappho goes on a journey in search of her
through the most miserable sections of many towns and
cities (surely a kind of Underworld or Land of No Return). Sappho is distracted in her quest by meeting
Phaon (the name of the man who, legend has it, was
loved by the poetess, Sappho). For a short time, she
imagines that she can deny her own quite masculine
nature and simply give way to her feminine urge to
abandon herself and submit. She "kills" Attys by
tearing up the letter she received from her which gave
her address and said she would return. Phaon, however, is searching for the same abandonment, and by
donning Attys' clothes, shows that he too wishes to
assume a submissive role. In despair, driven beyond
her limits, Sappho leaves Phaon and determines to commit suicide. She is rescued by a net (an image associated with Isis) like someone who has almost drowned.
This ending, clearly suggestive of a passage through
the waters, or death, to rebirth is the final symbol
of these tales. Sappho has realized that her story
too will repeat itself, because anyone she loves will
be Attys. She is therefore reborn to a new knowledge

of herself and to a more general, and therefore more impersonal, understanding of her role. She has sacrificed her child to attain the wisdom that allows her to evaluate her life.

The same desire for self-knowledge and integration of the self into all of human experience, which is characteristic of the third stage of the rites, is what prompted the writing of **Feux**. In it the author uses the myths of the race, as the shamans did. She examines love, looks more deeply into the problems and solutions of its mythical representations, and tries to go beyond the pain caused by the ending of one love to realize the positive value of an experience in which the human merges with the divine.[13] The **pensées** may be said to have this search for meaning as their principal role. They pose questions, comment on the previous story, prepare the reader for the one to come, and provide thematic links among the tales. They tell a story in themselves, but they are not primarily narrative. They are used to point up, by lyric passages, irony, sudden shifts in tone, etc., the meaning that can be lost in the tales should the reader become too involved with their specifics. By their use as commentaries and as links in a balanced structure that sets in relief the dangers and values of this experience, they represent the uniting of the masculine and feminine principles which alone can bring order, meaning, and a measure of self-control to the individual.

Love, as the adoration of an individual, has already been equated with death: "A god who wants me to live ordered you to stop loving me...In your arms, I could only die" (Pl 1079; E 45). The final section (Pl 1135; E 130) affirms acceptance, not only of life itself ("I will not kill myself"), but of her responsibility for what she has done and will do with it ("Let no one be accused of my life"). It summarizes her experience in love itself and what she has gained from it. "One can only raise happiness on a foundation of despair. I think I will be able to start building." The ironic twist to the second sentence of this maxim is indicative of emotional distance and

---

13. See Marguerite Yourcenar's Introduction to the 1957 (Plon) edition, p. 3.

61

wisdom already gained. The **pensées** close with a resolve not to be limited, even by despair, but to continue to **go beyond** the personal and the particular:
"It's only a question of beating a record." Such a
process of experience, and reflection upon it, became,
as Marguerite Yourcenar states in her introduction, "a
stage of awareness" (Pl 1049; E xxii).

Feux, then, is a book of lyrics--intricately related, subtly written--which demands the reader's in-
tense participation.None of the individual parts takes
on its fullest meaning unless it is seen as contribu-
ting to the structure of the book as a whole. This
whole, in turn,must be viewed as one step in a process
of becoming that did not end when **Feux** was finished.

Note on Nouvelles Orientales

Nouvelles orientales 'Oriental Tales' is, after **Denier du rêve**, the work of Marguerite Yourcenar that has changed the most from edition to edition. Like **Denier du rêve** and **Feux**, they make of myth a reality in modern times. There are scenes in **Nouvelles Orientales** that remind the reader of the dream sequences in **Feux**, **Denier**, and **Les Songes et les sorts**.

The stories in this volume fall into several groups. Those from the Far East are "Kâli décapitée" 'Kali Beheaded,' first published in 1928 based on a Hindu legend, and "Comment Wang-Fô fut sauvé" 'How Wang-Fo was Saved,' a Taoist fable. Balkan or Slavic tradition supplied the subject matter for "Le Lait de la mort" "The Milk of Death," "Le Sourire de Marko" 'Marko's Smile,' "La Fin de Marko Kraliévitch" 'The Death of Marko Kralievitch' (which was not written until 1978), and "Les Emmurés du Kremlin" 'Prisoners in the Kremlin' (omitted after the 1938 edition). The other stories are original, although "Le Dernier amour du Prince Genghi" 'Prince Genghi's Last Love' was written to fill the page left blank in Lady Murasaki Shikibu's **Genji Monogatari**.

L'Homme qui a aimé les Néréïdes," translated as "The Man Who Loved the Nereids," illustrates the living presence of legend or superstition in twentieth-century Greece and "Notre-Dame-des-Hirondelles" 'Our Lady of the Swallows' is an imaginary recreation of events that might have accounted for there being a chapel of that name in Attica.

Finally, there are two stories that had their names changed. "Les Tulipes de Cornélius Berg" 'Cornelius Berg's Tulips' became "La Tristesse de Cornélius Berg" 'What Saddened Cornelius Berg.' The ending of an unwritten novel, this story has little to do with the East, but does agree with the other stories in tone. "Le Chef Rouge" 'The Red Head' of 1938 became "La Veuve Aphrodissia" 'Widow Aphrodissia,' lest anyone should imagine that its French title referred to communist underground activity. Inspired by a short news item, it is both poignant and grandiose in its imagery and is probably the best of the collection.

Although they begin and end with stories about artists and how their art shapes their lives, these oriental tales are primarily about love. As in **Feux,** the theme of love is treated from many different points of view: love that turns to hate, maternal and married love, love as shown by service,love that rises above the routines of daily lives and provides a link with the eternal.

These stories, through their various revisions,appear in five editions from 1938 to 1982, besides pre-printings or re-printings in journals. The first edition was in Gallimard's collection "La Renaissance de la Nouvelle" under the direction of Paul Morand, in 1938. The second, revised and with a postscript was published in 1963; the third in 1975. The fourth, with a new story included, appeared in 1978. Finally they were included in their definitive form in the Pleiade edition of Marguerite Yourcenar's prose fiction. The book has also been translated into three languages. Only "The Man Who Loved the Nereids" and "The Milk of Death" have appeared in English.

This essay is theme-oriented and compares a figure from **Feux** with the most memorable character found in **Nouvelles Orientales.**

Antigone Twice Retold

Myths (and myth-making) occupy a central role in Marguerite Yourcenar's fictional world, especially in those works written in the 1920's and 1930's. They have been her "props through time."[1] Some are evoked directly in a variety of genres: prose poems, verse, and drama ("Antigone," "Endymion," and "Electre," for example).[2] Others are once removed from the original: characters in the 1934 **Denier du rêve** are compared explicitly to mythological ones, while still retaining their specific twentieth-century reality. Still others are further displaced, and exist as a substructure, revealed only to readers attentive to the author's use of image, theme, linguistic patterns, and literary devices.

We propose to show, first, ways in which Yourcenar's prose poem "Antigone ou le choix" 'Antigone or The Choice' resembles and differs from Sophocles' account. We shall then look at some elements of an original short story by Yourcenar, "La Veuve Aphrodissia" 'Widow Aphrodissia,' and suggest that its heroine is an Antigone figure.[3] In "Antigone," Yourcenar uses the plot and characters as we know them from Sophocles. Yet there is, in her rendition, a decided shift in emphasis in the treatment of some of the fundamental themes. Law and order, for example, is common to both works. Sophocles stresses a ruler's dilemma when the demands of the state and of the gods seem to be in

---

1. **Feux** in **Oeuvres romanesques** (Paris: Gallimard, 1982). All references to the novels will be to this Pléïade edition. **Fires,** trans. Dori Katz with the collaboation of the author (New York: Farrar, Straus, and Giroux, 1981). Pl 1043; E x.

2. Found respectively in **Feux, Les Charités d'Alcippe,** and **Théâtre II.**

3. Found in **Nouvelles Orientales,** included in the Pléïade edition.

65

opposition. His Creon judges all men by their relations with the state and fears anarchy above all
things. Antigone, as Jebb points out, is anarchy
personified.[4] Yourcenar conveys this theme by the symbol of the red flag. Her Creon "sees red" (Pl 1077; E
141), as though Antigone's bloody clothes were a flag.
In the Athens of Sophocles' time, law and order was
only beginning to be questioned as a value. For the
most part it was assumed that human law and the justice of the gods (**dike**) were one and the same. In the
mid-1930's,however, the tyrant is an unmitigated evil.
Yourcenar's Creon rests on the "hard pillow" of reasons of state (Pl 1078; E 42), and there is no question of his being right.

Opinions differ on the extent to which Sophocles'
Antigone is motivated by religious duty, since it is
discussed only briefly in the early part of the play.
In broader terms, however, Antigone's burying of Polynices may be considered a sacred duty since, as Kitto
notes,it was thought, in Sophocles' time, that elemental human forces were in themselves "divine."[5] The
question of whether Antigone or Creon is right is further compounded by debate over wisdom, i.e., whether
Sophocles conceived of it as **phronein** (the observance
of due bounds) or whether he understood it to be obe-
dience to human laws only until such time as they con-
flicted with the divine. Those who subscribe to the
first view (among them, Norwood)[6] consider Antigone
just as wrong-headed as Creon. Those who adhere to
the second (among them Jebb[7] see Antigone as right
in her decision to resist Creon and to obey divine
law. Kitto, too, supports the idea that Antigone is
on the side of the gods and offers as proof the

---

4. Richard C. Jebb, ed., **Antigone** (Cambridge: at the
   University Press, 1902), p. xxvii.

5. H.D.F. Kitto, **Form and Meaning in Drama** (London:
   University Paperbacks, 1960), p. 177.

6. Gilbert Norwood, **Greek Tragedy** (New York: Hill and
   Wang, 1960), p.138.

7. Jebb, p. xix.

"miraculous dust" that allows them to second her reactions against the decree which she finds so offensive.[8]

While Yourcenar's story of Antigone reflects Greek humanistic ideals, it contains as well elements of Christian ethics. We should note in passing that anachronism in Yourcenar's myths is used to highlight her belief in the unity of humanity beyond the limits of time and space.

Christian values and symbolism reinforce the sense of the sacred found in Sophocles and allow Yourcenar to make an unambiguous statement on the rightness of Antigone's actions. Wearing a seamless garment and walking over the battlefield as Jesus walked on the water, she is a Christ figure (Pl 1076 and 1077; E 39 and 41). Charity, therefore, supersedes justice as the criterion for judgment.

In both Sophocles' and Yourcenar's recounting of the legend, Antigone is a virgin. Sophocles' Antigone, however, regrets not being able to marry Haemon, while Yourcenar's heroine rejects marriage by which she might give birth to conquerors. Virginity as a positive value is a further indication of a Christian orientation.

A closely related theme, common to Sophocles and Yourcenar, is the relative value of the rational and the irrational, the latter held to be more "feminine" and more closely connected with the sacred.

Sophocles' Creon fears being dominated by a woman, or, as Segal suggests, by the woman within his personality.[9] Antigone, on the other hand, insists on following the law (**nomos**) rather than Creon's decrees (**kerygmata**). She allies herself totally, therefore, with the gods, rejecting Creon's rationalism and becoming **autonomos** 'a law unto herself.' She is also

---

8. Kitto. p. 147.

9. Charles Paul Segal, "Sophocles' Praise of Man and the Conflicts of the **Antigone**" in **Sophocles; A Collection of Critical Essays,** ed. Thomas woodward (Englewood Cliffs, N.J.: Prentice Hall, 1966), p. 73.

willing to accept the consequences of such an attitude, that is, death.

Yourcenar's Antigone, too, is the antithesis of rational human response. She seeks her star "at the farthest reaches of human reason a star that can be reached only by going through the grave" (Pl 1078; E 42). Her compassion makes her water in the heat of day and a lamp at night (Pl 1077; E 41). Her affinity with the divine is explicitly stated, for, when Polynices' body is taken away from her, she seems to be upholding God (Pl 1077; E 41).

Although there is some change in emphasis with respect to Creon and Antigone, the principal difference between Sophocles' and Yourcenar's characters lies in the role played by the people.

Sophocles' famous speech on man, although not totally optimistic in the context of the ensuing tragedy, expresses the pride that Creon and the chorus take in the results of progress. The confidence and joy, inspired by their victory in battle remain the prevailing mood. On the other hand, Yourcenar paints a profoundly pessimistic view of the people. She sees them as possessing the "vile absolution that comes from punishing" (Pl 1076; E 40), of scorning anyone who is different, of trying to impose their values on everyone, of prizing material or political gain above all else, and of losing their humanity by so doing.

Antigone rejects all of these attitudes. She follows what she believes right, not as a reaction to others, but seemingly because it is natural for her. Yourcenar's version is based upon the premise, adopted by many critics of Sophocles, that Antigone represents the highest ideal of woman's love and devotion, coupled with courage and novelty, but it goes further-- postulating her as an example of charity and dedication for ages to come (Pl 1077-78; E 41-42). [10]

It is hard to imagine a woman more different from this ideal than Aphrodissia. She is a Greek peasant woman, wife of the village priest, who falls in love with a red-headed outlaw. She lies and steals for him, flaunts her adultery in front of her husband (whom

---

10. The words referring to time "hors du temps"
    'beyond time' were omitted in the English

Kostis later kills) and consents to the killing of
their illegitimate child. She must conceal her love,
even when the villagers hunt down and kill Kostis and
his followers, planting their heads on pitchforks bove
the village, and heaping their bodies near the
cemetery to be burned. Horrified at this outrage, she
approaches the body and discovers that Kostis has tat-
tooed her name on his arm. Panic-striken, she buries
the body in her former husband's grave, then decides
that she must rescue his head. A peasant farmer, mis-
taking the head wrapped in her apron for a stolen veg-
getable, gives chase, and Aphrodissia falls down the
mountain to her death.

Despite many and obvious differences, Aphrodissia
shares some basic traits with Antigone: she too is an
exile in her own society, follows the dictates of her
heart rather than the rules of her group, is revolted
by the threatened desecration of the body of a man she
loves and finally commits suicide.

The differences in the general values and circumstances of the three stories are more a matter of degree than of kind. The community's value system is
based, in Sophocles' play, on reason that serves to
advance civilization and on the justice of the gods;
in Yourcenar's "Antigone," it is on reason without
compassion and justice without mercy; in "Aphrodissia," it is on a set of religious and social taboos
with justice belonging to the strongest.

To this rigidly enforced system, Sophocles' Antigone opposes her personal conviction on the will of the
gods or, as Kitto believes, her instinctive horror at
the "Affront to our common humanity."[11] Yourcenar's
heroine helps the vanquished "as though defeat proved
the justice of the cause" (Pl 1076; E 39), while Aphrodissia, like the Greek Antigone, reacts instinctive-
ly to an atrocity.

All three are doomed to die. Sophocles' Antigone
is condemned in part, it is suggested, because of the
curse on the house of Cadmus, but primarily because
she places herself outside Creon's law, which his hu-
bris will not allow him to redefine.Yourcenar's Antigone is portrayed as a "victim of divine law" and is

_____

translation.

69

hated, perhaps, because of this "privilege" (Pl 1077; E 41). Aphrodissia dies because she has known freedom with Kostis and can no longer live under the tyranny of the narrow-minded.

Images and motifs provide points of comparison sometimes among all three Antigones, sometimes between two of the three.

Images of birds of prey that desecrate Polynices' body in Sophocles are repeated in Yourcenar's "Antigone," (Pl 1077; E 40), but are replaced by flies in "Aphrodissia" (Pl 1197). A particular bird, the eagle, is used negatively in Sophocles, for the Argives, to represent a powerful marauder defeated. In "Aphrodissia,"the eagle is positive and represents Kostis,wild, free, living high above the common level (Pl 1199). Dogs, who, like the birds, attack the unburied body, carry the same negative connotation in **Antigone** and "Antigone." In Sophocles the urn holds the libation to the gods, poured out three times to satisfy the rites of burial, and is understood in the invocation to Bacchus. In "Antigone" she **is** the urn, or vessel, into which is poured the "wine of a great love" (Pl 1077; E 40). Wine images are, however, also used negatively in the French text. Empty wine bottles mark the route the armies have traveled (Pl 1076; E 38), and Thebes is described as "sleeping off its crime" (Pl 1078; E 43). In "Aphrodissia" the village priest (one of the most adamant in the pursuit of Kostis) is "drunk with wine from the Mass" (Pl 1195).

The sun, in Sophocles, is used primarily as a positive image: at the play's opening it is "golden day's eye" (a new dawning or beginning for Thebes now that the war is over)'; for Antigone, it symbolizes the life she must leave. Only secondarily does it stand for light in the sense of understanding. The first burial was discovered by the light of dawn--the second occurred at high noon. This latter image is the one developed in Yourcenar's "Antigone," where the noon sun stands for too much reason with too little compassion;"hate weighs on Thebes like a horrible sun" (Pl 1075; E 37), making things dry and hard; "abysmal noon" is equivalent to madness (Pl 1078; E 42). In "Aphrodissia," the sun is,[12] as we have shown at some length in another study[12] a symbol of Kostis,

---

11. Kitto, p. 155.

the beloved. Aphrodissia, like Antigone, was abroad at noon, feeling that it was **her** time (Pl 1197). The others in the story are portrayed as being unable to tolerate the sun at its full strength (Pl 1199). They will come out of their houses "when the sun becomes tame" and will celebrate by lighting a bonfire (ironically compared to their "illumination") to burn the outlaws' bodies. This fire is an unnatural image since it is lighted with gasoline (Pl 1197). It is intended as a posthumous insult since this is the way that the villagers disposed of mules' carcasses, i.e., objects not worth the effort to bury.

The idea of stoning, another form of public disgrace, is, in Sophocles, the announced punishment for burying Polynices.This image is omitted in Yourcenar's account, but reappears in two forms in "Aphrodissia." The first is a hailstorm that occurs during the first meeting of Aphrodissia and Kostis (Pl 1194); the second is Aphrodissia's very real fear when she sees her name tatooed on Kostis' arm: "She saw herself being stoned--buried under rock" (Pl 1197). Likening the stoning to burial under rock reunites the three versions, since both Antigones were buried alive in an underground cave, carved out of rock.

The plague is an image that appears only in the Antigone stories. Sophocles calls the dust storm that blinds the guards a plague. In Yourcenar's "Antigone," there is a plague of hate (Pl 10075; E 37) that is equally blinding to the citizenry as a whole.

The list of images on which such comparisons could be made is long indeed.Among them are images of height and depth, lightness and weight, ascension and fall, and images of the tomb, the prison, or blood. All of these merit detailed study.

Elements of phraseology and description also serve to tie these three stories together. For example: the setting for Antigone's deed, Sophocles says: "The ground was dry and hard."[13] In Antigone" we read that

---

12.   "Title as Image in Marguerite Yourcenar's "Le Chef rouge"/"La Veuve Aphrodissia, **Romanic Review,** LXXIV, No. 2 (1983).

13.   **Antigone** in **The Complete Greek Tragedies,** vol.

their hearts were dry like their ground (Pl 1075; E 37). "Aphrodissia" contains wording identical to Sophocles' (Pl 1198).

The ramparts of Thebes begin a series of descriptive elements that assume proportionally greater significance from one story to the next. In Sophocles the ramparts are mentioned only as the high point of the city from which Capaneus fell, struck by a thunderbolt when he was about to set fire to Thebes. In Yourcenar's "Antigone" it is the point of intersection of two themes. It is the place where the women gather to watch the battle and scream with joy at every shot that fails to hit one of their own (Pl 1076; E 39). Here too the heads of the enemy are exposed. Antigone does not join in the women's rejoicing, and, when her own pale face appears over the battlements between two severed heads, we understand that she too will die, a casualty in this war. Of course, there are no ramparts as such in a small Greek village. In "Aprodissia," therefore, the women assemble in the village square to wait during the three-day hunt for Kostis. At every shot echoing through the hills they scream--Aphrodissia more loudly than the rest--as befits the widow of the much-respected priest (Pl 1194). Thus, in trying to be like the others, she is still apart from them. She acts as the leader she is expected to be, which only increases her anguish over the possibility of discovery and the loss of position that would entail. The outlaws' heads, impaled on pitchforks, are placed at the highest point of the village, beyond which there is only mountain and sky, thus creating the nearest approximation to the battlements of Thebes.

The closing lines of "Widow Aphrodissia" carry the principal images of the story to the cosmic and mythical level:

> The slope became steeper and steeper, the path was more and more slippery as though blood from the setting sun had made its stones sticky... The path was only a track now and the track a scree... Aphrodissia understood only

---

III, ed. David Greene and Richard Lattimore (New York: Random House, 1954), line 250.

that she had to escape the village, its
its lies, its gross hypocrisy, the long
punishment of one day being an old woman whom no one loved anymore. Finally
a stone broke loose under her foot and
fell to the base of the precipice as if
to show her the way, and the widow
Aphrodissia plunged into the abyss and
into the twilight, carrying with her
the head spattered with blood.
(Pl 1200-01).

It is through images like these that we see
Aphrodissia raised to a new level. She is not by
circumstances or nature, a heroine of Antigone's stat-
ure; not a member of the royal house in a ruling city,
but only a peasant woman in a small town in Greece;
not a pure virgin, but a woman nearly taken in
adultery; dedicated not to a warrior prince dead on
the field of battle, but to an unscrupulous outlaw
hunted down by a posse; inspired not by religious duty
and respect for the gods, but only, at first by fear
and horror, and then by love, Aphrodissia has in common with Antigone only her revolt against a society
whose actions she condemns and the capacity for loving
greatly.

Marguerite Yourcenar uses myths and legends not
only to preserve and make more applicable and accessible the great tales of our Western heritage, but for
at least two other reasons.First,they provide a way of
reaching absolutes which cross religious and philosophical lines. Secondly, by creating ordinary characters, like Aphrodissia,who have affinities with mythical ones, she demonstrates her belief that they, too,
participate in the divine.

The Essays:
The Work That Is--The Work That Might Have Been

Many of Marguerite Yourcenar's essays may be thought of as "footnotes" to the intellectual autobiography that is the corpus of her work. They allow her to explain, to place in context, and to plead questions and causes that arise in her fiction. Other essays explore different possibilities. They are the "road not taken," but they still afford us insight into subjects that have intrigued her and provide a forum for discussing them.

The "footnotes" furnish the kind of information on Madame Yourcenar that she hopes to discover about those on whom she writes: her library; the purpose of her work; her methods of approach to her subject matter; her angle of vision; her perspective on eternal questions; her insights into fields other than literature; and finally the current issues that she feels will have an impact on the future welfare of humanity.

For purposes of organization we have divided the "footnotes" into four categories of which the first, extending over a period of forty years, pertains to her own writings, particularly to her historical novels.

The earliest of these came out between 1929 and 1934--after Margarite Yourcenar had spent a number of years preparing her early version of a novel on Haddrian and a roman fleuve that was to cover several centuries of European history. Although both were temporarily abandoned while she turned to **Alexis** and other projects, three articles remain to show us the line of development that will lead ultimately to the works of her maturity.[1]

---

1. "Diagnostic de l'Europe," **Bibliothèque universelle et Revue de Genève**, 18 (1929), pp. 745-52; "Le Changeur d'Or," **Europe**, 29 (1932), pp. 566-77; "Essai de généalogie du saint," **Revue bleue**, 72 (1934), pp. 460-66

Some of their subjects, themes, and basic assumptions about literary form will remain, almost unchanged throughout her career. The admiration she expresses in "Le Changeur d'Or" 'The Gold Changer' for the merchant, whose personal risks allow the exchange of goods leading to the spread of civilization, will be echoed by Hadrian. The two dealers in gold, the alchemist and the banker, one striving to advance learning, one protecting his position and the status quo, will appear as Zeno and the Fuggers in **L'Oeuvre au noir**. Sympathy for the trials of the Jewish people, reiterated in **Archives du Nord,** refutes the charges of anti-semitism leveled against **Mémoires d'Hadrien** and **Coup de grâce.**2

The relationship between imagination, knowledge, and love that will lead eventually to her method of writing is sketched in 1934.3 But in this relatively early phase of her career, Marguerite Yourcenar's appreciation of history had not yet fully developed. In "Le Changeur d'Or" and "Essai de Généalogie du Saint" 'Genealogy of the Saint,' she speaks of the Alchemist and the Saint respectively. This tendency to generalize is also a trait of the 1934 version of **Denier,** where the characters are raised too quickly to the level of myth. It explains why she was not yet ready to move Hadrian from the embodiment of the Humanist Prince or Zeno from the Philosopher who was never wrong to the carefully delineated characters who come to life in her later works.

"Diagnostic de l'Europe 'Diagnosis on Europe'clarifies certain stylistic predilections that have puzzled some critics. In it she establishes early the relationship between lucid style and lucid thought, while condemning the overly personal and the careless style that often betrays subjective impulse rather than feelings which have been tempered by logic and discipline. Her readers are reminded of Father Cicca's monologue in "Rendre à César" deploring people's tendency to repeat "I, I, I" and of the underlying

---

2. Subsequent references to these and other novels except **Archives du Nord** (Paris: Gallimard, 1977) will be to the Pléïade edition.

3. "Généalogie," p. 461.

76

tendency to repeat "I, I, I" and of the underlying purpose of **Feux** which is to find a broader meaning behind personal experience by ordering and enriching them in such a way that they yield a lasting value.

During the 1950's and 1960's, the period of **Hadrien**, the revised **Denier**, and **L'Oeuvre au noir**, a new series of essays reveal the changes in Yourcenar's historical perspective. "Histoire Auguste" 'Historia Augusta' probes the validity of the sources on which a writer must depend.[4] The "Carnets de Notes de **Mémoires d'Hadrien**" "Reflections on the composition of **Memoirs of Hadrian**" (Pl 528; E 330-31) describe the method, based on St. Ignatius' spiritual exercises, by which she expanded her earlier beliefs about the imagination and record the reading, travels, and settings through which she reached out to Hadrian. "L'Ecrivain devant l'histoire" 'The Writer Confronting History' stresses twentieth-century man's need for contact with his past from which rapid change has seemed to alienate him. Here Marguerite Yourcenar traces the ways in which man has thought about and expressed his past; from myth to legend and example, to a humanism that makes history a vehicle for the study of man, and finally to what she calls the new humanism.

This new humanism sets human responses that are common to all times against an intricately detailed background depicting the scenes, the events, the intellectual, emotional, and moral climate of a given moment in the past. The authenticity of her settings (verified in notes and prefaces) allows the reader to judge how an historical character was conditioned by his circumstances and also to make a comparison with other times. The eternal elements permit a sympathetic understanding on the reader's part. Combining the emotion and psychology of the classical theater, for example, with the data provided by modern scholarship, the new humanism is intended to allow the reintegration of the individual with his past.

"Ton et langage dans le roman historique" 'Tone and Language in the Historical Novel,' (1972)[5] takes a

---

4. In **Sous Bénéfice d'inventaire** (Paris: Gallimard, 1962, 1978).

5. **NRF**, Oct. 1972, pp. 101-23.

retrospective view of problems already solved and responds to questions that no critic could ever answer definitely: e.g. why there is no conversation in **Hadrien**; how she verified every doubtful word in **L'Oeuvre** to determine its precise sixteenth-century meaning. Her discussion of the difficulties involved in achieving a suitable tone of voice in the past, since no model exists, leads to an analysis of how others have approached the matter and the reasons for her own choice—all of which helps in comparing Madame Yourcenar's works with those of her predecessors. The insights into Hadrian's character, deduced from the fragments available, afford the reader new means of participating in the finished work.

This essay is an excellent illustration of the extent to which Marguerite Yourcenar continues her interest in already published works and her willingness to share reflections on the creative process with her readers. While particularly true of her historical novels, it is not limited to them. The preface to **Feux** and **Denier** are similar to "Ton et langage" in that she has rethought influences and circumstances that had a bearing on their creation, has criticized or defended her decisions, and, in the writing the essays, has gained new insights into the creative works.

In this first category, then, we find articles which elucidate many phases of the creation of her historical fiction: the source materials she consulted; a comparison and evaluation of them; the deductive and sympathetic process by which she made her characters live; the questions she had to resolve while composing her works; her choice of style; and finally an evaluation of her own and her readers' attitudes toward her work. While her novels may be appreciated by many, these essays were written "for the few readers who may be interested in the genesis of a book" (Pl 838; E 361).

The second group of "footnotes" gives an expanded presentation of subjects that appear as underlying assumptions or as background in Marguerite Yourcenar's fictional work.

Art--painting, sculpture, and architecture--has been one of the primary means of access to the characters and beliefs of the people on whom she has written. The essay on Boeklin[6] shows the somber reflections underlying the three stories named for painters comprising **la Mort conduit l'attelage.**[7] More specifically, she gives her impression of Basel and Munster, two settings in **L'Oeuvre,** originally "D'Après Dürer" 'In Durer's style.' The interest shown here for the painters from the Middle Ages to the Baroque period also gives us a point of departure for discovering models for the successive layers that make up the mythological speakers in **Feux.**

All serious readers of Marguerite Yourcenar are aware of the extent to which another source, the Orient--its art, philosophy, and religions--permeate her work. Her admiration for the Chinese artists who try to paint the true nature of things makes clearer the art of Wang-Fo in **Nouvelles Orientales** (Pl 1139 ff) and her description of a world as yet uninhabited by man in the opening pages of **Archives du Nord** (pp. 13-18). Her preface to the **Gita-Govinda,** "Le Japon de la mort choisie" 'The Japan of voluntary death,' and **Mishima** all comment on the principle, basic to Marguerite Yourcenar's thought, of a unified creation and the intrinsic value of each of its creatures.[8]

Music, as well as the visual arts, is apparent throughout Marguerite Yourcenar's works, especially as it orchestrates great themes and is expressed by images of the dance. Two essays devoted to it, "Mozart à Salzbourg" 'Mozart in Salzburg' and **Fleuve profond,**

6. "L'Ile des Morts: Boeklin," **Revue mondiale,** I (1928), pp. 394-99.

7. Paris: Grasset, 1934.

8. Shri Jayadeva, **Gita Govinda,** trans. François di Dio, et. al., préf. Marguerite Yourcenar (Paris: Editions Emile-Paul, 1957); M. Yourcenar, "Le Japon de la mort choisie," **L'Express Magazine,** 1 mars, 1980. **Mishima** (Paris: Gallimard, 1980).

Sombre Rivière reflect her catholic taste.[9]

Dreams and myths are two other realms which Madame Yourcenar investigated extensively in the 1930's and which remained influential,but to a much lesser degree in her later works. In 1938, in her preface to **Les Songes et les sorts**, she states her personal views on the importance of dreams, the interaction between dreams and reality, the extent to which they can explain time, space, and matter as we know them. These ideas, on which much of the 1934 **Denier** and **Feux** are based, reappear in both **Hadrien** and **L'Oeuvre**. The architecture of dreams is of particular interest, as we read of the stairways of Lycomedes' castle in **Feux** (Pl 1063; E 19-20) and of those in Piranesi's engravings[10] The three articles entitled "Mythologie" 'Mythology' elaborate on the significance of such figures as Phaedra, Ariadne, and Clytemnestra and provide a link between the pictures found in **Feux** and the ones in her plays.[11] Even more importantly, however, they help to explain the relationship of the poet and myth and reinforce the feeling of the sacred, without which her mythological works would be completely misunderstood.

Not all of the "explanatory footnotes: are fully developed expositions on important topics; some are, instead, merely "suggested additional readings." Tibetan religious practices, for instance, are mentioned only in passing in the essay on Hortense Flexner.[12] Yet they can add new dimensions to themes or images in Marguerite Yourcenar's own works. The theme of sacrificing a sacrifice, for example, which appears more than once in **Feux** seems clearly to be related to the ritual of chod among certain lamas: the "red meal" of sacrifice is followed by the "black meal" during

9. "Mozart à Salzbourg," **Revue bleue,** 75 (1937), pp. 88-89. **Fleuve Profond, Sombre Rivière** (Paris: Gallimard, 1964).

10. In **Sous Bénéfice d'inventaire**, pp. 116-169.

11. **Lettres françaises,** avril 1944, pp. 40-46; "II," oct. 1944, pp. 33-40; "III," juin 1945, pp. 35-45.

12. **Présentation critique d'Hortense Flexner** (Paris: Gallimard, 1969).

which the initiate realizes that he has nothing and is
nothing an can therefore make no sacrifice.[13] Phaedo's
dance, in which he tramples the other Phaedo of his
youth, likewise bears a close resemblance to these
ascetics who proclaim, "I trample down the self."[14]
These comparisons are not ones that will occur naturally to most Western readers. In the same way,
mention of oriental statuary and of the lives of the
mystics suggest areas in which each reader must evaluate his own preparation and fill the lacunae in his
own experience.

The third type of essay clarifies Marguerite Yourcenar's angle of vision of the world, her approach to
eternal questions, a critical appraisal of what she
finds. The complexity of her work is due in large
measure to her building up a multi-layered picture of
a place, an era, a people. We know from reading the
"Carnets" for Hadrien and other documents that one of
her primary concerns is to prevent the intrusion of
the authors viewpoint on the characters'.Nevertheless,
when we read essays like "Regards sur les Hespérides"
'Views of the Hesperides,' "Ah, Mon beau château,"[15]
or Hortense Flexner, we discover how Marguerite Yourcenar went about constructing the vision of Rome seen
in Hadrien and Denier or the haunting image of Bruges
in L'Oeuvre.

"Regards sur les Hespérides"is particularly illu-
minating because it succeeds in creating, in the space
of only a dozen pages,an image of southern Spain showing the many strata that unite to make it a living
presence for the reader. From the poetic invocation
of the names by which it has been known, to a recounting of its tumultuous history, to personal memories

_____
13. See Alexandra David-Neel, **Magic and Mystery in
     Tibet** (New York: Penguin Books, 1971), pp.
     151-52.

14. David-Neel, p. 158 and Pl 1107.

15. **Cahiers du Sud**, No. 315 (1953), pp. 230-41; "Ah!
     Mon beau château," in **Sous Bénéfice d'inventaire**.

she has of it, Madame Yourcenar traces the principal characteristics of a land where East and West have combined from earliest times to create a distinctive culture. She notes the physical evidence of man's presence--his buildings, monuments, and works of art. Each one is appreciated in itself, as it compares with those of other places, and as it represents a spirit and a set of values peculiar to its creator. She observes natural phenomena too: geography and the implications that it has had throughout history, the flora and fauna, and, going beyond the visible, the mineral life beneath the surface.

Cataloguing details, however, cannot complete or explain her vision. She sees her subjects in more than one dimension. The macrocosm of what the Ancients thought of as the unknown expanse of the Atlantic reminds us of Zeno's meditating on this same ocean from his northern beach and of the various solutions that it suggested for his problems (Pl 766-67; E 268-69). The microcosm is perhaps best illustrated in the essay on Flexner, whose love for her island extended to the insects and lichens. Zeno's interest also reaches to the smallest objects and the magnifying glass that he has made is the occasion for a striking image in "L'Abîme" 'The Abyss," the central chapter in **L'Oeuvre.** Upon awakening, he sees in it what he thinks at first, is a new insect, but which is in reality his searching eye (Pl 704-05; E 191-93).

All of the preceding points of view cannot be seen in the same temporal framework, but rather require different rhythms to express them. First, there is the rapid rhythm of short-lived phenomena: seasons, plants, animals, events as they happen. In this category must be included individual human lives, which are short even when they include a sphere of influence, as Clement Roux shows in his monologue on fame (Pl 269-70; E 146-47).

Secondly there is historical time. The past, from whatever period it is viewed, does not appear to progress uniformly. Times of change and upheaval seem to move more rapidly than those characterized by stability and calm--even though these traits may be errors due to perspective or lack of evidence.

Thirdly, there is a sense of time grasped by a contemplation of the stars or the elements in themselves. The elements lend themselves to all three of these kinds of duration. Water, for example, may be seen as an immediate need or as the mirror for a particular sunset; or it may be the seas as man learned gradually to navigate and to explore them; or it may be the immemorial tides as they are depicted in **Archives du Nord** (pp. 14-18). From the mineral world, marble has served as both subject and image throughout Marguerite Yourcenar's career and is shown in all three time-frames. In "Charités d'Alcippe," an early poem,[16] we can see an extended treatment of its life and the poet's participation with it: first unquarried stone formed by heat and pressure; then the disruption caused by the work of the stone-cutter and the pride of the sculptor; then the period of history during which it is admired, while its form endures and its fashion is appreciated. Although a statue is perceived in its sculpted form for a relatively long time, it begins, almost as soon as it is created, to change. It erodes as the weather attacks it or begins to be destroyed, as tastes and ideologies change, as accidents precipitated by human events have their effects on the marble. With a speed determined by the particular set of circumstances, the elemental begins to triumph over the merely human as the marble reverts to its former state, no longer a product of human ingenuity but once again a part of nature. The period of its association with man is long in the historical sense, but very brief in the life of the mineral.

    This cyclical sense of time, seen simultaneously on the three different levels, finds what is perhaps its most striking image in the fountain in **Denier** (Pl 272; E 149-50). It is set in the middle of a Rome which Clement Roux compares unfavorably with the city he remembers from his youth and with the ancient city, represented by its ruins. Tradition links the fountain with the future, since a coin thrown into it assures that the traveler will return to Rome. But the statue of Neptune that ties it to the ancient city is slowly disintegrating and returning to its natural state of stone and water, recalling the elements that predate man. "Le Temps, ce grand sculpteur" 'Time, that great sculptor'[17] makes explicit the effects of

---

16. **Manuscrit autographe**, 24, nov.-dec. 1929, pp. 112-117; rpt. in **Charités d'Alcippe**, pp. 7-12; E pp. 9-13.

17. **Revue des Voyages**, No. 15 (1954), pp. 6-9.

time on works of art: it can destroy them completely or create an abstract--like the Victory of Samothrace --which shows the feeling or idea of the sculptor more clearly now that it has lost the features that limited it to the representation of an individual.

It is important to note that, while Marguerite Yourcenar places great emphasis on acute observation, on the accuracy of her facts, and the concepts and images that can be drawn from them, she does not limit herself to what she can discover by travel or reading. She is particularly attuned to experiences that go beyond the normal range of the mind and senses. Discussed in such essays as "Généalogie" and those on the Venerable Bede[18] and the **Gita-Govinda**, mystics, mediums, magicians, and alchemists play a prominent role also in her fictional work.

The two best developed examples are the mystic Prior and the alchemist, Zeno, but Hadrian was also drawn to those able to conjure spirits, to magicians and fortune-tellers, and to the mystic rites prevalent in his time. Madame Yourcenar's interest in the supernatural is revealed in her earliest works. In **Feux,** Mary Magdalene is a mystic; **La Nouvelle Eurydice** is concerned with re-establishing contact with a dead woman; magical occurrences are the norm in more than one of the **Nouvelles Orientales.** In Marguerite Yourcenar's books, as in ancient rituals, it is necessary not only to live the experience, but also, in order to reach the highest stage, to remember to ask "What does this mean?" The constant search for transcendence, for for the meaning beyond perceptible reality is one of the primary characteristics of her work.

Her essays also allow her to present her viewpoint on basic human problems with which the protagonists struggle in her fictional world. The relationship between the soul and the body, an unresolved question in **Alexis,** is elaborated in the introduction to the **Gita-Govinda,** where Madame Yourcenar refuses either to scorn the flesh or to neglect the spirit, but rather shows

_____

18. "Sur quelques lignes de Bède le Vénérable" 'On a few lines of the Venerable Bede,' **NRF,** avril 1976, pp.1-7.

that the first is one means of elevating the second. Her commentary on this legend of Krishna, demonstrating the identification of the beloved with god and love as a means of attaining the highest spiritual plane, could serve as a philosophical basis for **Feux** and for "Saeculum Aureum" in **Hadrien** which treats Hadrian's love for Antinous (Pl 404-51; E 153-211).

The theme of suicide, introduced in **Le Jardin des Chimères** (1921) and in almost every subsequent work, but receiving its most important expression in **L'Oeuvre,** is one on which there is a great deal of disagreement on philosophical and psychological grounds. "Japon" (1980) in which Marguerite Yourcenar discusses the heroic aspects of the decision to die free leaves no doubt that she aligns herself firmly on Zeno's side in his decision to kill himself in prison rather than accept his sentence to die at the stake.

It is not only on major questions that the essays can help Madame Yourcenar's readers to judge or to validate their judgments on her fictional works. They can also serve as touchstones for determining her sympathies for certain characters. Her tendency to prefer the independent idealist to the conservative who protects the status quo, for example Marcella as opposed to Giulio or Oreste in **Denier,** however understandable the latter's problems may be, is clearly seen in "Changeur d'Or." The role of the small group that fosters the individual's growth or gives him emotional support is to be found in "Généalogie" as well as in many of her novels (**Denier,L'Oeuvre**), plays ("Electre"),[19] and short stories ("D'Après Rembrandt"). The essays are, therefore, an integral part of her work, reflecting the same preoccupations and underlying the continuity of her basic values.

Marguerite Yourcenar's view of life may in large measure be explained by her carefully cultivated ability to see, feel, and think as another, a goal set forth as early as 1934 in "Généalogie." Here too she describes the work of a creative genius as the condensing of his soul into a concrete product that can serve as both example and testimony. Her own creations, however, are not the only example nor the only

---

19. in **Théâtre II.**

testimony that she provides. Her sympathetic union
with others has made of her an outstanding reader,
critic, and translator.

Her article on the Venerable Bede presents us with
a model of the way in which she reads a text and may
serve as a blueprint for her readers to adopt. The
essay comments on two pages of the two-volume work[20]
Where Bede recounts a debate over whether or not to
allow a Christian missionary to preach in a pagan
country. Its central image--a bird that flies through
a dining hall in winter--symbolizes the brevity of
man's life and a respite between the storm and the
unknown on either side.

The importance of the incident is enhanced by historical and geographical information and by a study of
the language used in the various versions that have
come down to us. The historical debate is used as a
springboard for a discussion of people's attitudes toward and expectations of religion and the role it has
played in their lives, a subject taken up again in **Archives du Nord** (e.g. pp. 21, 28-33).Her commentary is,
perhaps, more striking than the original, for Bede was
writing an enormous work and had to move on quickly.
Marguerite Yourcenar, however, can afford to linger,
to see the scene with a poet's eye, to discover the
background that will enhance the image. She has done
what willing, careful, well-informed readers should,
but so often fail to do.

Marguerite Yourcenar's ability to put herself in
another's place leads naturally to the kind of involvement with the world that we find in the last
group of "footnote" essays. In these she speaks directly for causes which arise in her fiction, to be
sure, but rarely with direct reference to the twentieth century. Among these are: overpopulation,
cruelty to animals, crowded housing conditions, un-
healthy working conditions, and,most importantly, conservation and social justice.

----

20. Baedae, **Opera Historica**, trans. J. E. King
(London: William Heinemann, Ltd. and Cambridge:
Harvard University Press, 1962), i, pp. 283-85.

Conservation is approached obliquely in the article on Empedocles. While this ancient Greek protested water pollution, his primary focus was on man as an integral part of nature. In the introduction to translations of Oppianus of Syria, the positive view--that the more we know about nature, and especially animals, the greater is our attachment to them--dominates.[21] On the other hand, her letter against slaughter of baby seals castigates the supporters of this current outrage for the ignorance, greed, indifference, conquetery, or brutality that allows its continuation.[22] These characteristics, wherever found, or however displayed, are always condemned in any of Madame Yourcenar's works.

Fleuve Profond, Sombre Rivière, intended primarily to introduce its readers to Negro Spirituals, those "authentic masterpieces" [23] which she places among the great human witnesses" (**Fleuve** p. 63), is marked by the same assiduous attention to historical and sociological detail that we have noted in her other articles and in her novels. The careful evaluation of responsibility is also typical of Marguerite Yourcenar, who never places blame exclusively on the commonly accepted culprit. She analyzes the problems from various vantage points and attempts to show that our interdependence means that the blame must be shared by a much larger segment of society than would like to admit its involvement. Through her study of this one people, she shows the sympathy for the oppressed--both individuals and groups--that has formed the basis of so many of her novels.Whether the oppression be political, e.g. the dictatorship in **Denier,** or racial, e.g. Hadrian's predecessors' treatment of the barbarians, religious,e.g. the suppression of the Anabaptists in **L'Oeuvre,**or social,e.g. Alexis' alienation

21. "Empedocle d'Agrigente," **Revue générale,** 106 (1970), pp. 31-46; "Animaux vus par un poete grec" 'Animals seen by a Greek poet,' dec. 1970, pp. 7-11.

22. "Correspondance," **Le Monde,** 2-3 mars (1969), p. 12.

23. "Chants Noirs" 'Black Songs,' **Mercure de France,** No. 315 (1952), p. 251.

from his family and group, Madame Yourcenar has been on the side of the persecuted and an advocate of their right to protest.

The second category of essays--those on the work that might have been--gives us only tempting glimpses into other books and other fields to which Marguerite Yourcenar might have chosen to devote herself exclusively. She herself has said that there were many vocations that she might have followed.[24] Some of these, as we see in her essays, are: literary critic, art historian, translator, and classicist.

Her articles on literary criticism demonstrate the extensive and diversified background in the literatures of many cultures essential for sound judgments free from prejudice or parochialism. Her admiration and love for particular authors and literary forms have encouraged her to be an unashamed popularizer of them. One of the primary reasons for publishing **La Couronne et la Lyre**[25] was to present the Greek poets in such a way that they would be free from the stuffy atmosphere of the classroom and able to speak directly, on a human level, to twentieth-century readers. Her articles on and translations of Hortense Flexner, Constantine Cavafy[26] and the Negro spirituals seem to be motivated by the same spirit of sharing with others what had been a moving and meaningful experience for her.

In most of her literary essays, Marguerite Yourcenar tries to give, in addition to the special qualities of the writer, something from his times or situation that will be of lasting value for the reader. In the essay on Agrippa d'Aubigné it is a feeling of the desperate turmoil of the Renaissance, of a persecuted religious group; in Cavafy, the Greek world as shown in

----

24. In "Radioscopie," an interview with Jacques Chancel, 13 juin 1979.

25. Paris: Gallimard, 1979.

26. "Présentation critique de Constantin Cavafy," in **Sous Bénéfice.**

a modern soul and the problems of a man who differs
from the norm in his society (a subject dealt with
also apropos of Gide); in Mann, it is the psychological and philosophical problems of twentieth-century
man.[27] Almost all of the essays have some traits in
common with the others: a combined biographical and
thematic approach, extensive comparisons, a personal
response, but also some orientation or subject that is
peculiarly its own.

Her commentaries on Boeklin, Piranesi, and Rubens,
in which she aims more at discovering the soul behind
the paintings than at discussing their relative merits, attest to her long-standing interest in art and
her sensitivity to it. These essays may be considered
fragments of the work she would have done had she chosen to became an art historian by profession.

Her classical studies, especially **Hadrien**, which,
as we know, received the Prix Femina Vacaresco, a prize
given for essays, and **La Couronne et la Lyre** have received high praise from those who are classicists by
trade. These tempt us to imagine other studies on
other ancient Greeks and Romans who are our own favor-
ites and to regret that they are only works that might
have been.

Marguerite Yourcenar has often given the reasons
why she does not choose contemporary topics, or the
milieus in which she lives, for her fiction. Nevertheless, in the preface to "La Petite Sirène" 'The Little
Mermaid' she does give us some insight into how she
could have handled such a topic.[28] She paints the city
of Hartford where she lived during the Second World
War. She shows us its advantages, its strengths, its
prejudices, a few of its characters--

_____

27. **"Les Tragiques** d'Agrippa d'Aubigné" 'Agrippa
    d'Aubigne's **Tragédies,**' in **Sous Bénéfice**; "André
    Gide re-visited," in **Cahier André Gide** No. 3 (le
    Centenaire) (Paris: Gallimard, 1972); "Humanisme
    et hermétisme chez Thomas Mann," in **Sous
    Bénéfice**; "Humanism in Thomas Mann," trans. G.
    Frick, **Partisan Review**, 23, spring 1956, pp.
    153-70.

28. In **Théâtre I** (Paris: Gallimard, 1971).

some with rich personalities, other narrow in their
views--and a few bits of conversation for the tone.
This essay hints at the Yourcenarian regional novel
that might have been.

Finally, in the essay "Jeux de miroirs et feux
follets" 'Mirror Effects and Wills-o'-the-Wisp,'[29]
whose purpose is to trace the relationship of an
author with her characters, we find a book which she
seriously considered writing, for which she did research, but which was later abandoned. It was to be
on three Elizabeths: Elizabeth of Hungary, Elizabeth
of Austria, and Elizabeth Bathory (a saint, a melan-
choly beauty, and a witch). We have already discussed
Madame Yourcenar's interest in religion, politics, and
magic, but this essay is not on such a general level.
Instead she combines in one essay contacts that she
established with characters who do in fact appear in a
published work (the Berlaimonts of **L'Oeuvre**) with
those contemplated for the three Elizabeths, and, in
this way, gives us clues to her methods of writing
that should allow us better to appreciate the fictional works that she has written. In it we see first
how a complex interrelationship of interest in a region, attraction or fascination with a type of character,chance happenings, and the perception of a presence unexplained by any of the above can mesh to make
a character live for her. Secondly we learn something
of how she goes about finding the details that will
stimulate her own imagination and allow her to communicate the results to the reader.

The essay does not assume an important place in
the corpus of Marguerite Yourcenar's work until after
the Second world War. There are no doubt several reasons for this. In the first place she finds it by far
the most difficult to write, requiring more time in
research in proportion to the length of the finished
piece and causing, especially in the case of modern
writers, anxiety lest an injustice be done them. Secondly,essays are frequently the result of an editor's
request, and, since the publication of **Hadrien**, such
requests have increased dramatically.

_____

29. **NRF**, mai 1975, pp. 1-15.

It is not only in quantity, however, that change
has occurred. One very noticeable trait of Marguerite
Yourcenar as a writer is a tendency to blur the dis-
tinctions among the genres. Prose poems, a novel that
some consider an essay (**Hadrian**), and, with **Le Labyrinthe du monde**, an autobiography that includes elements of the essay, the novel, and poetry. It is not
surprising then, that in the essay she comes to util-
ize many of the same artistic techniques that she had
been perfecting for the other genres. Humor, irony,po-
etry, and the imaginative elements necessary for creating a literary character come to enhance her essays.

At the same time, enthusiastic readers of Yourcenar's novels began more and more to want to know the
author behind them, to discover her and her opinions,
to request, in other words, "footnotes" to explain
further the ideas that intrigued them in her fiction.

It appears that the essays improve in direct ratio
to the amount that Marguerite Yourcenar's imagination
in engaged in the project. Her essays on other writers, for example, seem more compelling the more she is
actively involved. The essay on the Venerable Bede
where she re-created his image, or the essays on those
whose works she has translated tend to move the reader
more than those in which analysis alone is used. The
best of the essays: "Bède le Vénérable," "Jeux de miroirs," "Ton et langage," "Le Temps," and certain of
her prefaces rival some of the fictional works in
interest.

As a group, the essays have an importance beyond
the information they contain. They bring out continuity in a body of work often characterized principally
by its diversity, while, at the same time, showing the
modifications that Madame Yourcenar's attitudes have
undergone. They also emphasize her desire--or even
her need--to be understood with the same degree of exactitude with which she has written. This tendency did
not develop until the 1950's as can be seen by comparing essays, and particularly prefaces, written before
and after that time. This may be another factor in the
essay's having become a more significant part of her
work in the last thirty years. At the start of her career they represented an opportunity to formulate the
thoughts that she was not yet ready to cast in fictional form. Later they provided occasions for the
arduous task of re-thinking and defining her ideas,

thus allowing her to understand her work more objectively. They also served as a means for her to crystallize those experiences which will not become books, but which have expanded or clarified her views of the world.

From Siren to Saint

As the first woman elected to the French Academy Marguerite Yourcenar would seem to be in an excellent position to be the outstanding feminist voice in French letters. She has refused. Opposed as she is to particularism of any kind, she must needs reject bias based on sex.

Her critics, though, have all too frequently become so caught up in their analyses of her male protagonists--Hadrian, Zeno, Alexis, Eric--that they have ignored the rich and varied women characters who people her books and have conveyed the false impression that Madame Yourcenar has neglected women to write exclusively about men.

We propose to give an overview of the major categories of Yourcenar's women characters, progressing from negative to positive, and to point out those qualities that make them women of character or nonentities --heroines or monsters.

The title "From Siren to Saint," reflects the very traditional dual view of women held, for example, by the unworldly Canon Campanus for whom every woman is "both Eve and Mary, she who yields to the serpent and she who gives her milk and tears to save the world." 1

Between these extremes, however, are to be found women of all types: from peasant to empress, from devoted mistress to hard-headed realist, from passive object to political activist. They are taken from ancient legends, from well-known myths, from history, from the creations of other writers, and from life itself. They represent many countries (of Europe, the Levant, the Orient) and many ages (legendary time, classical Greece and Rome, the Renaissance, the twentieth century).

---

1. **L'Oeuvre au noir** (**The Abyss**) Pl 582; E 34. All quotations from novels, except **Archives du Nord** and **Souvenirs pieux** will be to the Pleiade edition.

Not all of them are protagonists. A realist herself, and an historian, the author has had to rely on male characters to portray a great sweep of events. But the women's importance is not to be measured in direct ratio to the space they occupy, but rather by their influence and by their example.

The only women characters in Madame Yourcenar's first published work are mythological embodiments of a certain type of femininity: passive, resistant to change, promising a love likened to death. They are a negative force, tempting Icarus to abandon his aspiration to conquer the Chimera, to rise above his situation, to identify with Helios. These creatures, like the sirens in the poem "The Alms of Alcippe" (1929) lack a heart of their own to experience real emotion and rely on cliches of love.2

The woman as object, a phenomenon that Marguerite Yourcenar is amazed to find tolerated in the advertisements of women's magazines, is perhaps best exemplified by Angiola di Credo in **Denier du rêve**. Driven by her ambition to be a Hollywood star, Angiola attracts, uses, and then casts off a succession of people. Her life is valid only as a school for the actress. Finally, she has exploited her self to such an extent that Angiola Fides, her stage persona, is more real than the person.

Not temptresses,like Angiola, but equally destructive, are a small number of women in Yourcenar's works who can be considered basically evil. Some, like her Electra, based on Euripides' version of the myth, pay for their crimes with their tragic end.3 Of the others, the two most condemned by the author are Martha Ligre in **L'Oeuvre** and Noémi in **Archives du Nord**.

Martha is implicitly condemned by the contrast with her father, the saintly Simon Adrianson, and with her nurse, Johanna,who, though cold and harsh, has the

2. **Les Charités d'Alcippe et d'autres poems (The Alms of Alcippe)** pp. 7-8; E 9.

3. In **Théâtre II**.

virtues of strength,loyalty, and fidelity to her beliefs. Incapable of real love, Martha recognizes her
own abject fear and disgust when called upon to nurse
the dying Benedicta who has been a sister to her. This
failure, along with her renunciation of her reformed
faith, which is also a potential danger, haunt her all
her life. In compensation,she bends all of her efforts
toward achieving "success" in the material sense. The
description of her rich home, Forestal, almost unique
in Yourcenar's work, stands in ironic contrast to the
emotional and spiritual poverty of its owners.

Martha and her husband refuse to use their influence to save from the stake her half-brother,Zeno (who
as a physician treating victims of the plague wit-
nessed her cowardice at Benedicta's deathbed). On the
same morning Martha decides to embellish her house
still further by profiting from"a wonderful opportunity"--namely the sale of the confiscated goods of a man
unjustly executed for his political views. The tapes-
tries she thus acquires will increase in value and
will produce "a truly noble effect" representing as
they do biblical scenes: **The Worship of the Golden
Calf, St. Peter's Denial, The Burning of Sodom, The
Scapegoat, and The Jews Thrown into the Fiery Furnace!**
(Pl 812;E 329).

Noémi, Yourcenar's paternal grandmother, whom she
remembers, is as attached to things as Martha ("Close
the door of my livingroom. What time does it say on
my clock?); 4 is as anxious to protect herself as
she (As an old woman she left the house without seeing
her daughter-in-law who was suffering from puerperal
fever--which could not possibly be a real danger to
her.); and is as cold-hearted (When a neighbor heard
that she had died of heart-failure, he cried: "Her
heart! But she certainly never used it very much.")5
She is judged just as severely: "a prototype of
meanness." 6

---

4. **Souvenirs pieux** (Monaco: Editions Alphée, 1973).,
    p. 15.

5. **Archives du Nord,** p. 180.

6. **Archives du Nord,** p. 179.

Besides Noémi,there are other wives who make their husbands find excuses to remain away from home: Sabina (whom Hadrian would have divorced had he not been emperor); Giuseppa (who, after thirty years of marriage, still reminded her husband that he had taken her to a place where it had rained all during their honeymoon) (Pl 417; E 169 and Pl 178; E 19).

Marriage is an institution for which Marguerite Yourcenar has the highest of standards, and years of observation have shown her how many marriages fall short. Only occasionally is there a grudging word said for it: "When you talk about a hearth, sometimes you are talking about burning coals."7

Hadrian, as well as the good Canon, sees women as having two facets. The one, the matron (cold, proud, economical, concerned with her children and her household); the other, what he calls the "tender idols" of men who love women. These are the women who display to the greatest extent both the appearance and the characteristics of traditional"femininity." They tend, Hadrian notes, to be more concerned with display-- paint, perfume, clothes--than with qualities of the mind or spirit (Pl 333-35; E 60-65).

Vanity, or too much emphasis on dress,is often indicative, in Yourcenar's novels, of a weak character, passive and devoid of fervor whether for another person, a cause, or an ideal. Hilzonda, Zeno's mother,is an example of this type. The heavy brocaded velvets and jewels are reminiscent of a Flemish portrait, but beneath the clothes,we have trouble finding the woman. She is seduced by Zeno's father, leads an exemplary Christian life while married to Simon Adrianson,but is as easily led in the opposite direction when he is absent. She succumbs to the flattering attentions of Hans Bockhold at Munster, participates in his debaucheries, and dies by the executioner's axe when the city falls.

Weakness in women characters may be only relative by comparison to the men around them, or it may be due

---

7. **Archives du Nord**, p. 80.

to their nature or upbringing. Miss Jones, the timid
young Englishwoman of **Denier**, seems to be unable to realize herself as a woman. She is unaccountably terri-
fied of all men, and of Italian men in particular, feeling comfortable only in the bland company of her
friend, Gladys. A certain type of upbringing can dictate virtually unquestioned allegiance either to political authority, as is seen among the law and order
factions in **Denier** and **Archives**, or to God's will, especially as it is manifested through the church. This
submission is illustrated by the worshippers in Santa
Maria Minore of **Denier** and by the prayers of the piti-
ful Aunt Prascovia in **Coup de grâce**, whose weakness is
accentuated by extreme old-age. The author's opinion
seems to be conveyed in the image of her silver icon,
whose eyes of precious stone have been stolen by in-
vading soldiers, with the result that Aunt Prascovia
is praying to a blind protectress (Pl 96: E 24).

Some forms of weakness are not the result of either character or environment, but are rather a degree
of powerlessness dictated by social and economic
forces. Lina Chiari, the prostitute in **Denier**, has a
relatively small sphere of influence, but that does
not prevent Marguerite Yourcenar from seeing her good
qualities. Lina treats each of her clients with cour-
tesy and tries to meet his particular needs while he-
roically supressing her own. In a state of servitude
from which she will be released only by her approaching death from cancer, she confines her dreams to the
night and allows neither her fears nor her desires to
intrude on others' lives.

The large majority of women learn, if not to overcome, at least to cope with the condition allotted
them. A long succession of women, especially in **Le
Labyrinthe du monde** has given birth, often to far too
many children, raised those who lived, kept the home,
baked the bread, often worked with their husbands, protected the family's interests, nursed the sick, tended
the dying and waked the dead. Often they themselves
died prematurely as a result of their difficult lives.
Marguerite Yourcenar sees all of these nurturing and
protecting acts as "infinitely sacred," i.e. as con-
tributing to the cause of humanity.

As a group these practical women form a very significant part of the women in Yourcenar's work. As
individuals they represent many countries and social
classes. The solid, competent mistresses of the house

in **Labyrinthe** belong here, as does Wiwine of "D'Après Dürer" and **L'Oeuvre**. An orphan girl in her uncle's home, she is pious and hardworking, tending to the house and the church. In her romantic youth she falls in love with Zeno and promises to wait for him and wear his ring. Grown older and more "serious" she becomes an excellent housekeeper and cook. The ring, the author tells us is still on her finger, but invisible because of other rings--of fat.8

Old Mother Dida represents the hard life of the peasant.Although limited in her understanding of both, Dida does her duty to God and country as she sees it-- and the way that she sees it makes one of the most amusing and touching passages in **Denier** (Pl 250-61; E 119-134).Some consider her a harsh and grasping woman, yet she is secure in her self, her life, and her memories. She sees her harshness as coping with the realities of a far from easy life and her acquisitiveness as a sensible provision for a future for which she can count on no one but herself.

There are other women, often humble, often playing a small role in a novel as they do in life. They ask and receive little, but are still able to reach out to others. In **L'Oeuvre**, for example, the woman of Salzburg who gives Zeno bread when he is in need, could,he realizes, equally well throw a brick at him if the occasion demands. His old servant, Greete, expresses her love through shared memories, mended clothes, and food when Zeno is in prison. She also accepts risks to smuggle out a wanted man whom she does not know at all --in a disinterested act of charity.

Marcella, in **Denier**, is one of the most idealistic and one of the most well-rounded of all of Marguerite Yourcenar's women characters, playing the roles of daughter, wife, friend, and disciple. Her decision to assassinate the dictator is inspired by a desire to avenge her father who died in prison and by her attachment to a revolutionary leader as much as by her belief that the head of state in Italy in 1933 is evil.Now that Carlo Stevo,the theorist of their group, has been silenced, Marcella will attempt her coup,

---

8. "D'Après Dürer" in **La Mort conduit l'attelage** (Paris: Grasset, 1934), p. 82.

partly so that Carlo's work will continue, partly in
despair. Although she is determined on this move (la-
beled by another as suicide), she is nonetheless tempted to return to her husband whom she still loves and
is moved by half-romantic, half-maternal feelings for
Massimo, the young double-agent. Her death during the
failed attempt, which some might term futile, is her
witness and the result of her tragic affirmation of a
belief in individual protest.

Above all other qualities that her women characters may possess, Marguerite Yourcenar places the
capacity for love. Whether the love is maternal, romantic, abstract, or mystical; whether the woman is a
servant, friend, wife, lover, full partner, idealist,
or saint; love transfigures a woman and allows her to
transcend her position, time, and space. Even though
they may be rejected by the person they love and
serve, as Monique of **Alexis**, Rosalia, of **Denier**, and
Sophie, of **Coup de grâce** are, their devotion raises
such women to the rank of heroine.

It is in **Nouvelles Orientales** and **Feux**, where love
is the primary theme, and where there are the largest
number of women protagonists, that we can most easily
find a wide selection of different kinds of women who
love. There is Sappho, the acrobat, who is both lover
and mother to her young friend, Attys; Aphrodissia,
who, as we have seen, prefers to die protecting her
lover's body from desecration rather than to live in a
rigid society where her love is unacceptable; the Lady
-of-the-village-of-falling-leaves, who humbly devotes
herself to nursing the aging Prince Genghi, asking no
reward but a place in his memories.

There are also heroic women. Antigone carries
love for her family to an exemplary level of abstract
devotion to charity and justice. Mary Magdalene, although beginning at a very physical and immediate emotional level, rises through love and service to an understanding of the qualities of soul and the means of
salvation obtainable only through self-denial and sacrifice. These last two, on the symbolic level, under-
lie a number of other women characters in Yourcenar's
work.

The nymphs in "L'Homme qui a aimé les Néréides"
remind us that love is divine and that a human being
touched by this divinity will be forever changed by
it. The Oriental legend of Kali, in which a goddess'

head is attached to a prostitute's body, shows the highest and the lowest forms of love and comments on how much can be learned from desire, and from regret.

If there is a higher form of love, it is, as the persona of **Feux** says, "complicity," or partnership (Pl 1051; E 3). Lena, the servant and mistress of the Roman conspirators Aristogiton and Harmodius, gives unstintingly, yet is denied the reward of being completely accepted. Under torture (when the conspiracy has failed) she cuts out her tongue to avoid the shame of having to admit that she knows nothing, since she is not a fellow-conspirator.

This close relationship, the highest level of "earthly" love, if we may put it that way, is best exemplified by Plotina in **Hadrien** and the Lady of Froso in **L'Oeuvre**. These women are capable not only of love, love, but of active participation. They can under-understand the goals of Hadrian and Zeno and can contribute to their work. Both men, when dying, summon up the image of the one whom Yourcenar calls, significantly, their **parèdre** (a statue, representing the consort, which shares the niche or the altar with a god). By this term she indicates both the high value she attributes to this relationship and the ideal of equal sharing between a man and a woman.

The last step, already illustrated by Antigone, Mary Magdalene, and Kali, is the saint, who goes beyond the love of an individual to a love for God or a vision of the No-thing into which everything is absorbed. These women are capable of a more perfect charity and understanding than are ordinary persons. This level is represented by the Virgin Mary in the short story "Notre-Dame-des-Hirondelles" 'Our Lady of the Swallows,' in **Nouvelles Orientales**, whose vision rises above pettiness or fanaticism, and a woman such as Valentine, in **Anna Soror...** whose piety is matched by her wisdom which allows her to warn against, but not to try to interfere with what she sees as inevitable.

Even though we have given only selected examples of each category, it must still be clear that, far from ignoring women, Marguerite Yourcenar has portrayed them with varied characteristics, in all times and in every stratum of society. She has tried to see their strengths and weaknesses, both as individuals and as a group.

Yourcenar believes that women, who are closer to birth and to death than men, and who have tradition- ally been responsible for the preparation of food, the care of children and the home, may also be closer to the fundamental realities of nature, may place a high- er value on an individual life and on the quality of that life, may be capable of greater sensitivity and greater compassion. If, however, they become avid for material gain, more concerned with appearances than reality, and more self-centered than giving, then they will have given up their advantage.

All women are judged on the same basic criteria and, in fact, on much the same criteria as men in Mar- guerite Yourcenar's work. An unlettered servant who has the virtues of humility, simplicity, generosity, and loyalty, is judged better than her proud, incon- stant, and pretentious mistress. Each individual is honored for fulfilling her own potential and for being a force for good in her own sphere of influence, how- ever great or small that may be. Those women with the necessary intelligence, status, or power, must work to correct political, social, or religious oppression in the world. The others may set a smaller, but no less worthy example.

In terms of elemental images, which play a large role in Madame Yourcenar's work, women are primarily earth and water, the nourishing and sustaining ele- ments; while men are primarily fire and air.

The progression we have seen here shows a movement from those who are most self-centered or self-seeking and either hostile or indifferent to the needs of others, to those capable of great love, devotion, and sacrifice. In the second group a further distinction is made for those who devote themselves to a person or cause expecting no reward. It is this last type, the ones who can, in the words of **Feux** quoted before "give their sacrifice," that Marguerite Yourcenar most ad- admires. (Pl 1073; E 33). They are the ones who become exemplary characters.

Marguerite Yourcenar's women have not been falsely romanticized, their importance has not been exaggera- ted out of proportion, but neither they nor their causes have been either slighted or disparaged. They exhibit the same traits as women we all know. They cope with life's difficulties, succumb to its lures, and, on occasion, rise nobly above it. On the whole,

they   struggle with temptations, resolve to do better,
sometimes   stoop   to   being   sirens,   but aspire to be
saints.

The Art of Rewriting

> The friends that have it I do wrong
> When ever I remake a song,
> Should know what issue is at stake:
> It is myself that I remake.

Yeats[1]

Marguerite Yourcenar, like Yeats, is convinced of the value of rewriting her works, published and unpublished, and, like him, has not been lacking in critics to tell her that she is wrong. But her readers greet a new edition as enthusiastically as they do a new book. They know that she will have rethought and often recreated the work.

Some critics have been surprised that she should spend her time with subjects now grown old, and, they imagine, stale. Others deny that authors can bring the same zeal and freshness of viewpoint to a previously published work that they can to a new one. Still others claim that since a finished work is in the public domain, the author no longer has any right to alter it. But there have always been those who have admired her patient and persistent search for the exact emotional nuance, **le mot juste**, the most precise expression of her thought.

Throughout this theoretical debate, in which Madame Yourcenar has participated, sometimes with relish, sometimes in exasperation, she has continued to act on her conviction that rewriting is a valuable exercise that will enrich the book and reward both author and reader.

The emphasis that she has come to place on this practice demonstrates a shift in her view of herself

---

1.

William Butler Yeats, "Untitled," in **The Variorum Edition of the Poems of W. B. Yeats,** eds. Peter Allt and Russell K. Alspach (New York: The Macmillan Company, 1957), p. 778.

and of her duty as a writer. When she was twenty, Marguerite Yourcenar has confided in **Souvenirs pieux** (p. 213), her ambition was to be known, to an exclusive circle, as the anonymous writer of a half-dozen sonnets. This youthful and romantic notion did not last long, as she goes on to say. Yet she continued, throughout the 1930's to write hermetic literature which, if not deliberately obscurantist, at least did not eschew the cryptic and was readily accessible only to the initiated. The author of the 1936 edition of **Feux** accepted as inevitable that those who did not have "the key" were not "destined to understand." The author who, around 1950, was searching for ways to bring the Emperor Hadrian to life in a book, acknowledged with real regret that the truer the picture she drew, the less wide its appeal would be[2]

She has come, in short, to the view that it is her artistic responsibility to make what she believes to be important understandable to a wider audience. What she intends can be discerned in her essays (including her prefaces) and in interviews she has granted. How she implements her ideas may be gathered from a comparison of her earlier with her later works, but is made especially apparent through a study of the variants occurring in the different editions through which a given book has passed.

We shall consider three major categories of decisions that Marguerite Yourcenar makes in the course of rewriting: to refocus her perspective, to make stylistic revisions, and to reaffirm positions which, after reflection, seem to her basically valid. The examples we shall use are illustrative only. They could easily be multiplied.

The need to refocus the perspective on a book, character, or theme may arise from any one of several contingencies. Marguerite Yourcenar, as she has stated many times, considers that some characters do not reveal themselves completely to an author on first acquaintance. Of Hadrian she says in the appended **Carnets** (Pl 521; E 322) that such a subject should not be

_____

2. Pl 535; E 339. References to the definitive forms of the novels in French will be, unless otherwise noted, to the Pléiade edition, 1982, even though the changes occurred for the first time in an earlier edition.

attempted before the age of forty, because it is not possible before that to attain a proper perspective. In general, she believes that a "sympathetic magic" which allows an author to see and feel as someone else will produce the truest picture. This act of becoming another clearly necessitates time and a variety of experiences that are not available to a young writer.

Besides Hadrian, the best example of this process is Zeno, the alchemist/philosopher of a short story in **La Mort conduit l'attelage** in 1934. While rereading this volume for a new edition, she was once again convinced that Zeno was a crucial character, and from the fifty-page tale grew **L'Oeuvre au noir,** published in 1968.

"Artists in our times," says André Gide, "sin most frequently through their very great lack of patience. What is served up to us today, would often have been improved by being allowed to mature (**Corydon,** 1925, p. 8).

Some subjects are especially in need of distance from the primary material in order to permit the de-desired tonality. **Feux** is a particularly good example of such a subject. An outgrowth of an unhappy love-affair, **Feux** was intended as a vehicle for going beyond the purely personal in search of the universal. It is instructive to see what was added to the **pensées** (nothing was subtracted) between their prepublication in a journal and the appearance of the book less than a year later.

She can be reconciled to the end of such a love, now perceived as a form of death: "A god who wants me to live ordered you to stop loving me...In your arms, I could only die" (Pl 1079; E 45). she is more able to see herself as another: "Nothing dirtier than the ego" (Pl 1073; E 33), and salt has been added: "Wit? In grief? Why not, there is salt in tears" (Pl 1114; E 100). These differences can be attributed to her having gained a degree of detachment sufficient to allow her to deal objectively and even ironically with her own love.

The times also have their effect on a writer's work. It was the Second World War that deepened the tragedy in **Coup de grâce** (1939) and gave a nightmarish concentration-camp quality to the ship scene in "Qui n'a pas son Minotaure?" as well as providing the definitive viewpoint for **Hadrien.**

The relationship with her characters that we have noted is not complete ly severed once a book has been written. Besides the books that have been recast and the "Registry" at the end of "Rendre à César," where the end of each character's life is briefly described, we find occasionally that Marguerite Yourcenar has written a story from another point of view. Telling **Alexis** with Monique as the protagonist has tempted her more than once. The legend of the House of Atreus is recounted as Clytemnestra's problem in **Feux,** but as Electra's in the play named for her. Phaedra speaks in **Feux,** but she gives way to Theseus and Ariadne in "Qui n'a pas son Minotaure?" (**Théâtre II**).

Reader reaction is taken seriously by Madame Yourcenar, although it occasionally surprises and often disappoints her. In this case, we find her rewriting more in her notes and prefaces than in the works themselves. In a footnote to the printed version of her radio interviews with Patrick de Rosbo (**Entretiens radiophoniques,** 1972,p. 78), she chides her critics: "It is amazing that...[they] didn't hit on this solution by themselves. It's certainly the most plausible and the simplest, probably too simple for them." Explanations with regard to characters, themes,and background are, especially in the prefaces to **Feux** and **Denier,** attempt to orient the reader "correctly" to the work and correspond, one suspects, to comments by readers who have misunderstood it. The mere fact that from the 1936 to the 1967 edition, the prefatory note to **Feux** originally of one short paragraph expanded to an eighteen page preface is a revealing comment on the relations of writer and reader.

Yourcenar has been surprised by the emphasis critics have placed on the sexual preferences of some of her characters and also on what some of them have said (see Rosbo, pp. 77 ff). This is perhaps the reason she has chosen to de-emphasize the theme of homo- or bisexuality where possible. **Hadrien** and **Alexis,** based as they are on authentic models, could not be changed, but a minor fictitious character in **Denier** is not crucial and is modified. To reinforce the point that Miss Jones, the Englishwoman, is intimidated by men, the 1934 version makes her (discreetly in one or two sentences) a lesbian. In the 1959 edition, this allusion has been removed one degree and made only a hint: Miss

Jones' friend, Gladys, who is not a character in the novel at all, **may** have lesbian tendencies.

It must not be thought that Marguerite Yourcenar responds only to negative criticism. In the **Carnets** following **Hadrien** she thanks all of the "well-disposed readers" who have shared their knowledge and reactions with her and states her conviction that any reissued book is by way of being a cooperative effort between the author and such readers (Pl 539; E 344).

Some revisions are due to the fact that, with age, an author's perspective changes. The indignant sentence found in the 1957 preface: "**Feux** is not a youthful work; it was written in 1935; I was 32 years old" was modified in 1967 to read: "**Feux** is not strictly speaking a youthful work...." In **Coup de grâce,** "that man and that woman" later became "that boy and that girl." In the 1952 edition of **Alexis** she is less dogmatic than in the 1929 version: "absolutely pure" is softened by the addition of "(or what people see fit to call that)." Almost inevitably, the older author occasionally shows a less optimistic viewpoint: "But it seems to me that everything would be acceptable if only everything were understood" (**Alexis,** 1929, p. 36) has been suppressed.

Contemporary problems have occupied a progressively larger place in her work, perhaps in response to such critics as Jean Blot, who said in **Marguerite Yourcenar:** "Nowhere do we find her [Madame Yourcenar] neither herself, nor her environment, nor her condition, nor her country, no her times."[3] Had she answered directly, it might well have been in the words of Terrence: "Humani nil a me alienum puto." Instead, she seems, to some extent, to have retreated from the position expressed in the preface of **La Mort conduit l'attelage:** that it makes no real difference of what age one speaks, but that history affords us a better perspective.To some modern readers and critics, writing of war, poverty, greed, injustice, intolerance, etc., is not dealing with today's problems Unless the story has a modern setting. So she became more specific, as for example in the updated section of the **Carnets** (Pl 532; E 336) where modern housing

_____

3. 1971; rpt. Paris: Seghers, 1980, p. 9.

complexes are called "termitières" 'termite hills' and in **Feux** where the victims (1936, 1959) in an ancient Greek torture chamber became metaphorically "dying animals,"comparing them to the victims in vivisection laboratories (Pl 1087; E 58).

Character changes in rewritten works are nearly always for the purpose of sharpening the focus for the reader. in **Denier**, for example, of which she said that two-thirds of the 1934 version was discarded in the rewriting, two characters changed name. Rosa (1934) became Rosalia (1959), and Sir Junius Round (1934) became Sir Junius Stein (1959). In the first case, no doubt, the name was too common, allowed too many associations, and in the second too uncommon, too obviously a stereotype label. "Stein" gives the same basic feeling as "Round," that of a ponderous stability which would answer Angiola's needs, but the impression is more subtle. That this name change is not indicative of a change in attitude on Madame Yourcenar's part is proved by a slip of the tongue in the Rosbo interviews. She refers there to "Rosa," showing that her feeling toward the character is unchanged.

Of the central chapter of this book, the one concerning Marcella, large portions were changed between the 1934 and the 1959 editions. Passages comparing Marcella with other women and describing her as a wife and lover were considerably reduced in order to focus on her as a political force,since her assassination attempt is the central plot of the novel. No important element is eliminated, but the emphasis has shifted. As Madame Yourcenar indicates, "I say almost exactly the same thing, though sometimes in different terms." (Pl 162; E 170).

Occasionally, a character is slightly changed. One example occurs in "L'Homme qui a aimé les Néréïdes" (**Nouvelles Orientales**) apropos of a person mentioned only in passing. The mistress whose lover lost his senses after loving the nereids and who "wept two years before being consoled" (1938, p.77) is in no way the same as the woman of the 1963 version who "wept two months..." (Pl 1183).

In **Alexis** a more fundamental change is made in Monique, Alexis' wife. In the 1929 edition she, like her husband, is Catholic. In the 1971 version, she becomes a Protestant. In the light of the times in which this story was set, and in the light of the view of

Protestantism in other writings of Madame Yourcenar, we may posit that this change indicates a certain' independence of spirit that will allow Monique better to cope with her husband's desertion and with the receipt of the letter.

Stylistic changes are numerous in all of the books that have been reissued. The major importance of such changes is to convince the reader that the republication of one of Marguerite Yourcenar's books is no insignificant event to be authorized after a hasty rereading. Each thought, word, letter, punctuation mark is considered with regard to its effect on the totality of the work.

Many of the more striking stylistic changes may be attributed to one of two seemingly contradictory ends: to individualize or to universalize. Madame Yourcenar seeks to avoid stereotypes, vaguely defined individuals, or ones not integrated into a broad view of human affairs. To make each of her characters most fully himself, she has rigorously examined his characteristics, actions, and thoughts to find ever better ways of making him both unique and unforgettable. This was done, for example, in **Denier** by the addition of more telling details and by a more extensive use of indirect style,which allows a comment on a commentary.

Describing the life of a shop-keeper,Giulio: "During the war (1934, p. 38) became by 1959: "He had served in the army for four years during the war, and that hadn't been a bed of roses." (Pl 178; E 19). His wife had a lover who was "in every way" superior to Giulio, "even when it came to money." This was changed to"seeing that he had been decorated and owned a car." His wife drove away his shop assistant, the attractive Miss Jones, whom he had hired "out of sheer charity" (Pl 180; E 21). The "sheer" was added to emphasize the double irony, conscious and unconscious, implied by the author and the subject.

This same Giulio takes his place in history when he lights a candle, as many had done before him, because "they had found nothing better to offer them [the gods] than a little flame" (1934, p. 53). This image was strengthened to read:"century after century, they had surrounded their holy relics with an honor guard of tiny flames." (Pl 187; E 31).

Clarification is a constant concern. A reference to McCarthy, in an essay on Hortense Flexner [4] was expanded to "of the witch hunts," since he might not be recognized by her French audience. The "wheel-gods" of the 1938 **Nouvelles Orientales,** which may have been too cryptic, is enlarged to "gods with many arms and legs like wheels" (Pl 1203-04).

Practical problems also claim Madame Yourcenar's attention. Times and places are made more logical or more vivid to the reader. In the first version of **Electre,** [5] the conspirators spoke of the future's being only half an hour away--not a realistic time span for the play. This was changed, before it was incorporated into **Théâtre II** (1971),to "a morning" (p. 45). In **Denier,** Donna Rachele escaped from a besieged barn "through the orchard" which gave a less immediate and graphic image than the later "through an abandoned cistern" (Pl 195; E 43).

Shifts in viewpoint are another minor stylistic point to which Marguerite Yourcenar has given careful attention. For example in "Le Dernier amour du Prince Genghi," the woman sang a song "which she didn't much like, but which the prince loved dearly" (**Nouvelles Orientales,** 1938, p. 138). In the 1963 edition, the first phrase is eliminated to keep a single viewpoint. Likewise when Giulio is the subject of a description in **Denier,** "Vanna's daughter" of 1934 is called "his sweet little grand-daughter" to express more clearly her relationship to Giulio (1959).

Questions of fact are naturally rectified. A name, illegible in manuscript, was erroneously transcribed in **Souvenirs pieux** as "Feuillée." A reader wrote to suggest that Alfred Fouillée might be the man in question. The error was corrected and explained in a footnote in **Archives du Nord** (p. 360). An estimate made in **Présentation critique de Constantin Cavafy** (1958): "the break caused by Islam came seven centuries earlier in Alexandria than in Byzantium and Athens..." was changed in **Sous Bénéfice** to "eight centuries" (1962, p. 195).

---

4. NRF, 1 fev. 1964, p. 216.

5. **Electre ou la Chute des masques** (Paris: Plon, 1954).

Most of the changes would be noticed only by a comparison of textual variants. The stages through which they have passed, however, have produced editions remarkable for their precision, clarity, and striking imagery. Especially for dramatic moments in her characters' lives, Marguerite Yourcenar searches for the exact image to reveal their soul. It is not sufficient that Phaedra "does her best to believe that the rape really took place" (**Feux**, 1936, p. 17); "rapture by rapture, she imagines the rape Hippolytus will be accused of" (Pl 1054; E 7).

"In writing so as to be understood," said Ezra Pound, "there is always the problem of rectification without giving up what is correct." 6 If Marguerite Yourcenar is able to say of a work that "fell short by half (and not just half)"(**Théâtre II**, p. 178), she is equally capable of defending those aspects of it which she considers valid. Because of this, she has been criticized for infringing, in her prefaces, for exam-example, on the domain of the critic. This infringement, however, is surely more than compensated by the wealth of information received. Usually what is **not** changed in Marguerite Yourcenar's books will be defended by the author--this includes her style, her choice of subject matter, her deliberate omissions, her methods, her form, and her opinions.

Madame Yourcenar's style and form have varied,from the restrained and even severe language used in a classical **récit** like **Alexis** to the outpourings that the author categorizes as "baroque expressionism" in the lyrical **Feux**. Both of these styles have their critics; both have their advantages. Neither resembles the style used in the books written after 1950. Yet, not only has Yourcenar not made significant changes in their basic style when they have been reissued, but she has defended them as they stand as having inner coherence between subject and form and as being worthy expressions of their time (see prefaces: **Feux** Pl 1042-49; E ix-xxii, **Alexis** Pl 3-7).

---

6. Quoted in "Studies in 'The Cantos,'" ed. Marie Henault (Columbus, Ohio: The Charles E. Merrill Publishing Company, 1971), p. 4.

The role of myths (see prefaces to **Feux** and **Theatre II,** the problem of homosexuality as a suitable and necessary theme for literature (see preface **Alexis**), and political commentary in a novel (see **Théâtre I,** pp. 15-16) are some of the subjects on which she has answered her critics. Responses of this type constitute another dimension of Madame Yourcenar's work and are interesting in themselves as well as for the light they shed on her work.

Paradoxically, though she has been chided for speaking too extensively on some facets of her work, there are others where requests for information have been ignored or refused. Students of literature who so far forget their discretion as to ask of authors what they would blush to ask their friends have not had their curiosity satisfied.

Predictably, it has been on the subject of love that this reticence has been most apparent. In the preface to **Feux** written in 1967, Madame Yourcenar protests once more that love poems need no commentary and that while she knows that she is seemingly avoiding the question, it is because the question (on the experience that prompted the book) is not a valid one. In **Souvenirs pieux** (p. 239) she has tried to disarm critics in advance on the subject of her mother's adolescent attachment for a school friend, no doubt anticipating a struggle for information similar to the one over **Feux.**

We have said that Marguerite Yourcenar's rewriting came as a response to an evolving view of her role as a writer. In the more than sixty years from her first to her most recent book, the changes have been not so much in themes, most of which were announced in her earliest works, but in their treatment and in her relationship with her readers. Madame Yourcenar has come to feel responsible for assuming a greater share of the burden of communication. It is not enough to let him who will, understand. The writer must lead the reader--as she has done in her prefaces; must make her points absolutely clear--as she has tried to do in rewriting; must try to adapt to the form her audience understands best--in our era, the novel, a genre about which she has many reservations; must remember that books "are not always read, or well read" (Rosbo, p.8) --and use other means of communicating her message, such as newspaper and radio interviews.

In a word, the author must give more freely of herself. Marguerite Yourcenar has been accused, as we have seen, of being niggardly with respect to her personal feelings. Nonetheless, she has agreed to "participate...in those two dangerous pursuits, talking about oneself and talking about everything" (Rosbo, p. 7).

She has also resigned herself to becoming more direct. Instead of remaining with the assumption that the messages of history or myth are comprehensible to a sufficient number, she has applied herself to speaking more directly about the current manifestations of human prolems. It is interesting to note that the essay did not assume its present significance in her work until after she had taught in college. Surely it would be plausible to assume a connection between these two facts.

Alain Bosquet, in his article "Marguerite Yourcenar et la perfection"'Marguerite Yourcenar and Perfection',7 has attributed her rewriting to her respect for her readers. What we have just said would tend to confirm his views. Nevertheless, we believe that to be only partly the reason. It is also, and perhaps primarily, that an artist like Madame Yourcenar must continue to perfect her work in order to fulfill herself. Complacency is one of the cardinal sins on her personal list, after ignorance and injustice. It is one that she seeks strenuously to avoid.

The self-criticism that she admires in Yeats has become a way of life. She is her own most severe critic: "a book (if I may put it this way) infinitely botched" (Rosbo, p. 18). She requires herself to make incessant unobtrusive rectifications of nuances of which even careful readers are probably unaware: e.g. the last sentence of the Note to **Souvenirs pieux,** describing her attitude toward the characters in it was changed between the publication of a limited edition (of 500) in 1973 and the Gallimard edition only months later, in 1974.

A book published too soon, "inflicting perpetual remorse on its author" (Rosbo, p. 20) demands to be rewritten. She must do it whether or not her critics

---

7. **Livres de France,** mai 1964, p.3.

are satisfied, whether or not her readers believe they understand and are happy, whether or not honors and rewards are offered for the first version. Marguerite Yourcenar has evolved her own requirements. Her books are not finished until they satisfy her.

Chronology

1903 Marguerite de Crayencour (Marguerite Yourcenar)
     is born on June 8.
1914 A year spent in England.
1917 She begins to write poetry.
1919 She receives her **baccalauréat**.
1921 Her first book is privately printed.
1929 Death of her father Michel de Crayencour, Janu-
     ary 12.
     Alexis, her first published work, appears.
1937 She meets Grace Frick and makes her first
     trip to the United States.
1947 She becomes an American citizen and changes
     her name legally to Marguerite Yourcenar.
1950 With Grace Frick, she buys "Petite Plaisance,"
     her home in Maine.
1952 Prix Fémina-Vacaresco for **Mémoires d'Hadrien**.
1954 **Memoirs of Hadrian** receives the Newspaper Guild
     of New York's Page One Award.
1961 Honorary Doctorate from Smith College.
1962 Prix Combat for **Sous Bénéfice d'inventaire** and
     the body of her work.
1968 Honorary Doctorate from Bowdoin College.
     Prix Fémina for **L'Oeuvre au noir**.
1970 Election to the Royal Belgian Academy of French
     Language and Literature.
1971 Election to the Legion of Honor.
1972 Prix littéraire de Monaco.
     Honorary Doctorate from Colby College.
1974 Grand prix national de la culture.
1977 Grand prix de l'Académie française.
1979 Death of Grace Frick, November 18.
1980 Election to the Académie française, March 6.
     Promotion in the Legion of Honor.
1981 Reception at the Académie française.
     Honorary Doctorate from Harvard University.
1982 Election to the American Academy of Arts and
     Letters.
     A wildlife reserve, named for Marguerite Yource-
     nar, is opened near her childhood home.

Bibliography

Books by Marguerite Yourcenar
(in chronological order by first editions)

Le Jardin des Chimères. Paris: Librairie Académique, 1921.

Les Dieux ne sont pas morts. Paris: Editions Sansot, 1922.

Alexis ou le Traité d'un Vain Combat. Paris: Au Sans Pareil, 1929; rpt. Plon, 1952 and 1965; rpt. Les Cent-Une, 1971; suivi de **Coup de Grâce**, Gallimard, 1971; rpt. (Pléïade) 1982.

La Nouvelle Eurydice. Paris: Grasset, 1931.

Pindare. Paris: Grasset, 1932.

La Mort conduit l'attelage. Paris: Grasset, 1934.

Denier du rêve. Paris: Grasset, 1934; rev. ed. Plon, 1959; rpt. Gallimard, 1971 and (Pléïade) 1982. English: **A Coin in Nine Hands.** Trans. Dori Katz with the collaboration of the author. New York: Farrar, Straus, and Giroux, 1982.

Feux. Paris: Grasset, 1936; Plon, 1957 and 1968; rpt. Gallimard 1974 and (Pléïade) 1982. English: **Fires.** Trans. Dori Katz with the collaboration of the author. New York: Farrar, Straus, and Giroux, 1981.

Les Vagues by Virginia Woolf. Paris: Stock, 1937.

Les Songes et les Sorts. Paris: Grasset, 1938.

Nouvelles Orientales. Paris: Gallimard, 1938; rev. ed. 1978; (Pléïade) 1982.

Le Coup de Grâce. Paris: Gallimard, 1939; rev. ed. 1953; (Pléïade) 1982. English: **Coup de Grâce.** Trans. Grace Frick with the collaboration of the author. New York: Farrar, Straus, and Cahady, 1957.

Ce Que Savait Maisie by Henry James. Paris: Laffont, 1947.

Mémoires d'Hadrien. Paris: Plon, 1951; rev. ed. 1958; rev. ed. Gallimard, 1971 and (Pléïade) 1982. English: **Memoirs of Hadrian.** Trans. Grace Frick with the collaboration of the author. New York: Farrar, Straus, and Young, 1954.

Electre ou la Chute des masques. Paris: Plon, 1954; rpt. in **Théâtre II** Paris: Gallimard, 1971.

Les Charités d'Alcippe. Liège: La Flûte enchantée, 1956.
English: **The Alms of Alcippe.** Trans. Edith R. Farrell. New York: Targ Editions, 1982.
Le Mystère d'Alceste et Qui n'a pas son Minotaure? Paris: Plon, 1963. rpt. in **Théâtre II.**
Présentation critique de Constantin Cavafy. Paris: Gallimard, 1958; rev. ed. 1978.
Sous Bénéfice d'inventaire. Paris: Gallimard, 1962; rev. ed. 1978.
Fleuve Profond, Sombre Rivière. Paris: Gallimard, 1964; rev. ed. 1978.
L'Oeuvre au noir. Paris: Gallimard, 1968; rpt. (Pléîade) 1982.
English: **The Abyss.** Trans. Grace Frick with the collaboration of the author. New York: Farrar, Straus, and Giroux, 1976.
Présentation critique d'Hortense Flexner. Paris: Gallimard, 1968.
Théâtre I. Paris: Gallimard, 1971.
Théâtre II. Paris: Gallimard, 1971.
Discours de réception de Marguerite Yourcenar à l'Académie royale belge de langue et de littérature française. Paris: Gallimard, 1971.
Entretiens radiophoniques avec Marguerite Yourcenar. Paris: Mercure de France, 1972.
Souvenirs pieux. Monaco: Editions Alphée, 1973; rpt. Paris: Gallimard, 1974. First volume of **Le Labyrinthe du monde.**
Archives du Nord. Paris: Gallimard, 1977. Second volume of **Le Labyrinthe du monde.**
La Couronne et la lyre. Paris: Gallimard, 1979.
Les Yeux ouverts. Paris: Gallimard, 1980.
Discours de réception à l'Académie française de Marguerite Yourcenar et réponse de M. J. D'Ormesson. Paris: Gallimard, 1981.
Mishima ou la vision du vide. Paris: Gallimard, 1981.
Anna, Soror.... Paris: Gallimard, 1981; rpt. in **Comme l'eau qui coule.** Paris: Gallimard, 1982.
Comme l'eau qui coule. Paris: Gallimard, 1982; rpt. (Pléîade) 1982.
Oeuvres romanesques. Paris: Gallimard (Pléîade), 1982.